the Amish *of* Lancaster County

ALSO BY DONALD B. KRAYBILL

AMISH GRACE
How Forgiveness Transcended Tragedy
with Steven M. Nolt and David L. Weaver-Zercher

HORSE-AND-BUGGY MENNONITES
Hoofbeats of Humility in a Postmodern World
with James P. Hurd

AMISH ENTERPRISE
From Plows to Profits
with Steven M. Nolt

THE AMISH AND THE STATE

THE AMISH
Why They Enchant Us

WHO ARE THE ANABAPTISTS?
with C. Nelson Hostetter

ANABAPTIST WORLD USA

ON THE BACKROAD TO HEAVEN
Old Order Hutterites, Mennonites, Amish, and Brethren
with Carl D. Bowman

THE RIDDLE OF AMISH CULTURE

THE PUZZLES OF AMISH LIFE

THE AMISH STRUGGLE WITH MODERNITY
with Marc A. Olshan

the Amish *of* Lancaster County

Donald B. Kraybill

Photographs by Daniel Rodriguez

STACKPOLE
BOOKS

Published by
STACKPOLE BOOKS
5067 Ritter Road
Mechanicsburg, PA 17055
www.stackpolebooks.com

Printed in China

10 9 8 7 6 5 4 3 2 1

FIRST EDITION

Design by Beth Oberholtzer
Cover design by Caroline Stover
Map by Eberly Designs

Library of Congress Cataloging-in-Publication Data

Kraybill, Donald B.
    The Amish of Lancaster County / text by Donald B. Kraybill ; photography by Daniel Rodriguez. — 1st ed.
        p.   cm.
    ISBN-13: 978-0-8117-3478-3 (pbk.)
    ISBN-10: 0-8117-3478-1 (pbk.)
    1. Amish—Pennsylvania—Lancaster County—Social life and customs. 2. Amish—Pennsylvania—Lancaster County—Social conditions. 3. Amish—Pennsylvania—Lancaster County—Pictorial works. 4. Community life—Pennsylvania—Lancaster County. 5. Lancaster County (Pa.)—Social life and customs. 6. Lancaster County (Pa.)—Ethnic relations. 7. Lancaster County (Pa.)—Church history. I. Rodriguez, Daniel (Daniel Enoc) II. Title.
    F157.L2K725 2008
    305.6'89774815—dc22
                                                                    2007033212

Contents

Right: These girls are carrying homemade meadow tea
to family members baling alfalfa hay on a hot day.

The Amish of Lancaster County

Lancaster County, Pennsylvania, has enjoyed the reputation of being the Garden Spot of the World for many years. The Amish of the Lancaster area have contributed to the county's fine agricultural reputation. Their distinction as one of America's most colorful and interesting religious groups extends far beyond eastern Pennsylvania. Indeed, many of the 8.3 million tourists who travel to Lancaster County each year come to catch a glimpse of Amish life.

Although Amish people live in thirty-four Pennsylvania counties, about half of Pennsylvania's 57,000 Amish reside in Lancaster County, which hosts North America's oldest and most densely populated Amish settlement. The Holmes County, Ohio, area is America's largest Amish settlement, followed by Lancaster, with nearly 27,000 children and adults. About half of that number are under eighteen years of age.

In the early 1900s, Lancaster's Amish numbered only about 500. A century later, their population had grown to 27,000, with an additional 10,000 offspring living in Amish settlements outside the Lancaster area. The expansion of the Lancaster settlement mirrors Amish growth nationally. Now scattered in twenty-seven states and Ontario, the national population of children and adults numbers about 220,000. More than half of America's Amish live in Ohio, Pennsylvania, and Indiana, with some 1,600 congregations located in 370 geographic settlements.

Different Amish communities have different customs. Some non-Lancaster Amish forbid automatic milking machines, which are common in the Lancaster community. Amish in some other areas drive buggies with different color tops—black, yellow, or white—whereas the Lancaster carriages are gray. Many of the Lancaster Amish do not use power lawn mowers or ride bicycles, but these items are accepted by some other Amish groups. The Lancaster Amish have indoor plumbing and contemporary bathrooms. In sharp contrast, some of the more traditional Amish in other settlements use outdoor toilets. In general, the Lancaster Amish are one of the more progressive subgroups in their use of technology.

Despite the diversity, several common badges of identity unite Old Order Amish across North America: horse-and-buggy transportation, the use of horses to pull machinery, plain dress in many variations, a beard and shaven upper lip for men, a prayer cap for women, the Pennsylvania Dutch dialect, worship in homes, private one-room schools, and taboos on public electricity. These symbols of solidarity unite the Amish world and also mark its boundaries with the larger society.

Alfalfa is a major crop raised for hay to feed cows on traditional dairy farms. This farmer is raking dried alfalfa into rows to prepare for baling it the next day. Mules pull the rake.

Sprawling to the east and south of Lancaster City, the Amish community is organized into some 160 church districts, or congregations. Twenty to forty family units totaling, on average, about 165 adults and children constitute each district. Streams, fence rows, and roads form the boundaries of each district, the basic social and religious unit of the community.

Families participate in the church district that encircles their homes. The geographic size of districts varies with the density of the Amish population. In small districts, families often walk to the church services, which meet every other Sunday and rotate from home to home. As districts increase in members, they divide. A bishop, two or three preachers, and a deacon, without formal pay or education, share leadership responsibilities in each district. The district is church, club, family, and precinct all wrapped up in a neighborhood parish.

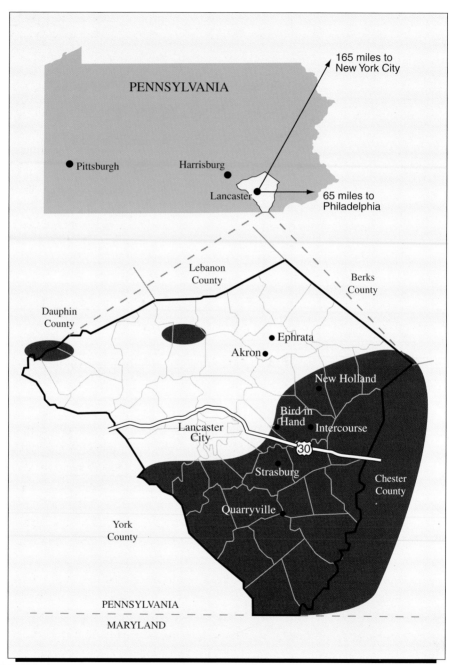

The Lancaster Amish settlement, concentrated in the dark areas on the map, includes western Chester County.

The Amish own private property and live side by side with non-Amish neighbors on farms, along country roads, and in small villages. U.S. Route 30 runs east and west through the county and divides the settlement physically as well as socially. Many of the church districts south of this route have a higher proportion of farmers and tend to be more conservative than those to the north.

Nestled in southeastern Pennsylvania, sixty-five miles west of Philadelphia, Lancaster's fertile acres face the steady press of urbanization. Indeed, the county has lost hundreds of farms in recent years. One of the fastest-growing counties in Pennsylvania, Lancaster is projected to gain 190,000 people between 1970 and 2010, swelling its population to 510,000. High land costs, growing suburbanization, and the continuing expansion of the Amish community have prodded some Amish families to head for other parts of Pennsylvania, Kentucky, Indiana, Wisconsin, and other states in search of cheaper farmland and rural isolation.

The Secrets of Amish Population Growth

Amish immigrants settled in neighboring Berks County before coming to the Lancaster area about 1749. Several more Amish congregations took root in Lancaster County during the nineteenth century, but they never flourished. Amish adults numbered fewer than 500 by 1900. The settlement prospered in the twentieth century, however, doubling every twenty years as well as planting new colonies in other areas of Pennsylvania. Since 1950, the national Amish population also has doubled about every twenty years. What are the secrets that propel their growth?

The Amish do not actively evangelize. They do welcome outsiders, but few are able to leap across the large cultural gap. Instead, growth is fueled by a robust birth rate that averages seven children per family, and about ninety-five percent of them join the church. In the Lancaster settlement, the dropout rate—adults who leave the Amish community or youth who choose not to be baptized—is less than 10 percent. Sizable families and the strong retention rate are two factors that propel Amish growth.

Children develop a strong sense of Amish identity at an early age by wearing distinctive clothing and speaking the Pennsylvania Dutch dialect.

Two other factors also have contributed to the growth of the Lancaster settlement: *cultural resistance* and *cultural compromise.* The Amish have resisted modern life by constructing cultural fences around their community. Badges of ethnicity, such as horse, buggy, lantern, and dress, draw sharp boundaries between Amish and modern life. Daily use of these symbols reminds insiders and outsiders alike of the cultural divide between the two worlds.

The Amish have resisted the forces of modernization in other ways as well. Cultural ties to the outside world are curbed by speaking the Pennsylvania Dutch dialect, marrying within the group, spurning television, prohibiting higher education, and limiting social interaction with outsiders. Amish schools insulate youth from the influence of worldly peers and reinforce Amish values. From birth to death, members are embedded in a thick web of ethnicity. These cultural fences fortify Amish identity and help abate the lure of modernity.

Cultural compromises also have enhanced growth. The Amish are not a calcified relic of bygone days. They are changing continually. Their willingness to compromise, to negotiate with modern life, often results in fascinating mixtures of tradition and progress. For example, Amish members are allowed to ride in cars but not own them; they can use phones but not install them in their homes.

In the context of Amish culture, these negotiated compromises are reasonable, indeed ingenious, ways of achieving community goals. Hardly foolish contradictions, they preserve core values while permitting selective modernization. The cultural compromises bolster Amish identity while reaping many benefits. Such flexibility boosts the economic vitality of the community and also retains the allegiance of Amish youth.

Thus in the final analysis, a combination of biological reproduction, cultural resistance, and cultural compromise has enabled the Amish to flourish and grow as a distinctive people in the midst of modern life.

Myths and Realities

Romantic images of the Amish abound in the American imagination. Popular myths portray them clinging to frontier ways—washing clothes by hand and cooking over open hearths. The Lancaster Amish do diverge from modern ways, but they also sip sodas, bounce on trampolines, and use in-line skates. Amish life offers a peaceful pace and pleasant satisfaction, but it's not idyllic. The sweat of toil and earnest struggles to harness social change lace their daily world.

Some popular images of the Amish are fiction; others reflect outdated Amish practices. This book seeks to replace the misperceptions with realities of contemporary Amish life. Consider some of the following myths.

Myth: The Amish are isolated from the outside world. They rarely interact with outsiders, whom they call "the English." *Fact:* Most Amish people in Lancaster County have non-Amish friends and interact with outsiders on a daily basis. The Amish often refer to outsiders as (the) English because they speak English rather than the Pennsylvania Dutch dialect spoken by the Amish.

Myth: The Amish do not change. They live like our ancestors did three or four generations ago. *Fact:* Amish society is continually changing. It changes more slowly than American society in general, but it is not a social museum. Windmills, for example, used for pumping water for many decades, have been replaced by other types of pumps on many Amish homesteads.

Myth: All the Amish are farmers. *Fact:* It is true that some Amish are farmers and that most Amish live in rural areas. Since 1980, however, many Amish

As occupations have shifted away from farming, many families live in newer homes with adjacent shops rather than on traditional farmsteads.

people have earned their living from nonfarm occupations. Indeed, nearly two-thirds of Lancaster's Amish households rely primarily on income from various types of nonfarm employment.

Myth: The Amish are ignorant and backward. *Fact:* The Amish do terminate formal education at the eighth grade and forbid high school and college attendance. They emphasize practical, vocational, and self-directed education. Though formal schooling ends with eighth grade, vocational training continues through apprenticeships. Hundreds of self-trained Amish entrepreneurs have developed some 2,000 successful small businesses in Lancaster County.

Myth: The Amish reject modern technology like the Luddites of nineteenth-century England. *Fact:* The Amish selectively use technology that is compatible with their values. They reject some things, such as television, but they have adopted other forms of modern technology, such as in-line skates, indoor plumbing, and gas barbecue grills.

Myth: The Amish are hypocrites because they use technology inconsistently. They refuse to own cars but will ride in those belonging to others, they have tractors at their barns but do not use them in the field, they use telephones but not in their homes, and so on. *Fact:* In order to survive in the modern world, the Amish have made many cultural compromises. These may look like inconsistencies to outsiders, but from the Amish perspective, such practices are logical adaptations as they seek to preserve their community in the face of the strong tides of modernization.

Myth: Amish women are oppressed by men, who control the rigid patriarchal society. *Fact:* It is true that women do not serve as ordained leaders in their church, but they do have a voice and vote in church business meetings. Many women operate small businesses and have freedom for creative expression as artisans in their homes and shops.

Myth: Amish youth are encouraged to leave home, live in cities, and explore the outside world during a period of *Rumspringa,* or "running around." *Fact:* Around the age of sixteen, young people join a youth group, but they do not leave home. They continue to live with their parents but participate in youth activities with their friends on weekends, when they do have new opportunities to explore the outside world.

Myth: Because the Amish are so old-fashioned, their communities are slowly dying out. *Fact:* The Amish population of Lancaster County grew rapidly during the twentieth century, doubling about every twenty years.

Myth: The Amish are self-righteous religious people who condemn the outside world. *Fact:* The Amish do not judge people of other religious persuasions. They believe that only God judges people. Moreover, they have a remarkable respect for other churches and do not believe that the Amish are the only people headed for heaven. In a spirit of humility, they seek to be faithful to the teachings of Jesus and the Amish church, knowing that God will be a merciful and just judge of their lives.

Religious Roots

Amish roots stretch back to the time of the Protestant Reformation in sixteenth-century Europe. In January 1525, youthful religious reformers in Zurich, Switzerland, outraged authorities by rebaptizing one another as adults. These dissenters declared that the New Testament had more authority over religious matters than the Zurich City Council, which insisted on the practice of infant baptism. In fact, rebaptizing adults was punishable by death at that time. The dissenters believed that baptism was appropriate only for adults who made a voluntary confession of faith. The radicals were dubbed Anabaptists, or rebaptizers, by their opponents, because they had been baptized as infants in the Catholic Church. The Anabaptist movement, sometimes called the Radical Reformation, quickly spread through the cantons of Switzerland and into Germany and the Netherlands, as well as other nearby areas.

Threatened by the rapid spread of Anabaptist groups, civil and religious authorities commissioned "Anabaptist hunters" to stalk the land. Not surprisingly, the first martyr was killed in 1527 by drowning. Over several decades, nearly 2,500 Anabaptists burned at the stake, drowned in rivers, starved in prisons, or lost their heads to the executioner's sword. The 1,100-page *Martyrs Mirror,* first published in Dutch in 1660 and later in German and English, records the carnage of the bloody theater.

The Swiss Anabaptists sought to follow the teachings of Jesus in daily life by loving their enemies, forgiving insults, and turning the other cheek. Some Anabap-

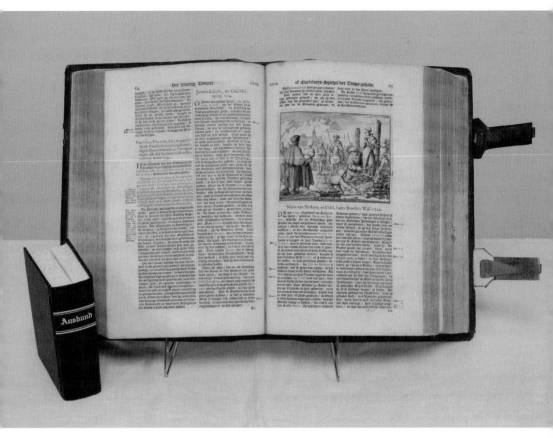

Two important books in Amish faith, in addition to the Bible, are the 1,100-page *Martyrs Mirror* and the *Ausbund,* the Amish hymnbook.

tist groups resorted to violence, but most of them resolved to live peaceably, even with their adversaries. The constant threat of execution, however, tested their simple faith in the power of suffering love. Some recanted, but many died for their faith. Obedient to the words of Jesus, they yielded themselves to God's will, even in the face of torture. Martyr stories continue to undergird Amish values today.

Harsh persecution pushed many Anabaptists underground and into rural hideaways. The sting of persecution reinforced the biblical teaching about a cleavage between the church and the larger society. In their eyes, the kingdoms of this world, which used coercion, clashed with the peaceable kingdom of God. The vision of creating a community unstained by worldly affections has animated Anabaptist hopes over the generations.

Many Anabaptists gradually assumed the name Mennonite, derived from a Dutch Anabaptist leader, Menno Simons, a prominent preacher and writer who converted to Anabaptism in 1536. About 150 years later, Jacob Amman, also a convert, became a leader in the Swiss Anabaptist church. Born in Switzerland, he moved to the Alsatian region of present-day France as part of a wave of Anabaptist emigration to avoid Swiss persecution. In 1693, Amman sought to revitalize the Anabaptist movement. He proposed holding communion twice a year rather than once, as was the typical Swiss practice. Influenced by Dutch Anabaptists, he argued that Christians, in obedience to Christ, should wash one another's feet in the communion service. To promote doctrinal purity and spiritual discipline, Amman forbade trimming beards and wearing fashionable dress. He administered a strict discipline in his congregations. Appealing to New Testament teaching and the practice of Dutch Anabaptists, Amman also advocated shunning excommunicated members. This issue drove a divisive wedge between his followers and other Anabaptists living in Switzerland and Alsace— a division that widened into a breach beyond repair.

Amman's followers, eventually known as Amish, developed their own identity in the Anabaptist family. As religious cousins, the Amish and Mennonites share a common Anabaptist heritage. Since the division in 1693, however, they have remained distinctive communities. When Amish and Mennonites arrived in North America in the 1700s, they often settled in similar geographical areas.

The Quilt Work of Amish Values

Lovely Amish quilts symbolize the patchwork of Amish culture—the memories, myths, and beliefs that shape the Amish world. *Gelassenheit* (pronounced Geh-lah-sen-hite) is the cornerstone of Amish values. Roughly translated, this German word means submission or yielding to a higher authority. It entails self-surrender, accepting God's will, yielding to others, self-denial, contentment, and a quiet spirit. The Amish believe that Jesus calls them to abandon self and follow his example of humility, service, and suffering.

This way of thinking—of yielding to God and others—permeates Amish culture. Children learn the essence of *Gelassenheit* in a favorite schoolroom verse:

I must be a Christian child,
Gentle, patient, meek, and mild,
Must be honest, simple, true,
I must cheerfully obey,
Giving up my will and way . . .

Another favorite saying notes that "JOY" means Jesus first, Others in between, and Yourself last. Amish teachers sometimes remind students that the middle letter of pride is I. In these ways, children are taught to hold others in higher esteem than themselves.

The spirit of *Gelassenheit* expresses itself in *obedience, humility,* and *simplicity.* To the Amish, obedience to the will of God is the cardinal religious value. Disobedience is dangerous, because it can lead to eternal separation from God. Acceptance of authority—parents, teachers, leaders, and God—creates an orderly community.

Obedience is coupled with humility in Amish life. Pride, the opposite of humility, is a religious term for unbridled individualism. Proud individuals display the spirit of arrogance, not *Gelassenheit.* The spirit of *Gelassenheit* collides with the bold, assertive individualism of modern life that seeks personal achievement, self-fulfillment, and individual recognition at every turn. What non-Amish people simply consider proper credit for one's accomplishments, the Amish view as the hankerings of a vain spirit. Proud individuals tack their name on everything, promote personal accomplishments, draw attention to themselves, seek recognition in the press, and want photos of themselves. Pride disturbs the equality and tranquility of an orderly community. The humble person freely gives of self in the service of community without seeking recognition.

Simplicity is also esteemed in Amish life. Fancy and gaudy decorations point to pride. Simplicity in clothing, household decor, architecture, and worship nurtures equality and orderliness. The tools of self-adornment—makeup, jewelry, wristwatches, and wedding rings—are taboo. To Amish eyes, these cosmetic props cultivate vanity and encourage individuals to show off. Whereas modern dress accents individual expression and social status, plain Amish dress signals acceptance of the collective order.

Children learn the value of hard work at an early age. Daily chores, which often involve caring for animals, contribute to the economic well-being of the family.

The Amish rejection of individualism most deeply separates them from modern culture. Amish culture esteems collective values over unbridled individual freedom. Bending to the call of community, however, does not smother individual expression in Amish life. Outside observers are often surprised by the amount of personal freedom in Amish society. What they lose by giving up the freedom of self-expression, the Amish gain in a durable ethnic identity and a caring, supportive community.

Compared with the frenzy of modern life, the Amish pace is slower. Even the battery-operated clocks on Amish walls seem to run more slowly. Regulated by the rhythm of the seasons, time expands and relaxes. From body language to the speed of transportation, from singing to walking, the pace is slower.

The Amish embrace a strong work ethic. Idyllic views of Amish life quickly fade in the face of hot and dusty toil. Cows are milked morning and evening, every day. Garden vegetables must be picked despite the sultry heat. Piles of dirty clothes from large families are washed and dried without the aid of electric dryers. But despite its harsh edge, work becomes a redemptive ritual in several ways. It is always a team effort, binding family and neighbors together. In Amish eyes, work is not a career, but a calling from God that enhances the common good. Work, usually done with others and often interlaced with play, contributes to the welfare of family and community.

Amish society pivots on a delicate tension between tradition and social change. In contrast to the consumer world, where new is always better, the Amish tilt toward the past. In the words of one member, "Tradition to us is a sacred trust. It is part of our religion to uphold and adhere to the ideals of our forefathers." Instead of embracing the modern assumption that progress always leads to a better life, "We ask," says one Amish man, "where will these changes take us? What will be the outcome of innovations?"

Amish values—obedience, humility, simplicity, hard work, and esteem for tradition—uphold their vision for an orderly and contented community. These are ideal values, however. As in all human communities, gaps appear between the ideal and the real. Greed lifts its head at times. Jealousy and envy sometimes flare. Rowdy youth occasionally embarrass community elders. Marriages can sour, and interpersonal feuds sometimes rupture community life. Beneath the patchwork of Amish ideals, these are indeed people who, like all humans, have their share of problems.

$\backsim$

Amish Spirituality

Amish spirituality has several distinctive features. It is grounded in the New Testament, especially Jesus' Sermon on the Mount, and the witness of sixteenth-century Anabaptist martyrs. Key written sources, in addition to the Bible, are the *Ausbund* hymnbook, the *Martyrs Mirror,* the *Dordrecht Confession of Faith* (1632), and various prayer books.

Amish spirituality has a communal rather than an individualistic accent. It focuses on a quiet and humble practice of faith. Nonviolence, nonretaliation, and love of enemies, based on Jesus' example on the cross, are central to Amish spirituality. The Amish reject the use of force, seeing it as a violation of Jesus' teachings. Reflecting their commitment to nonresistance, they do not join the armed forces or initiate litigation in court.

Forgiveness is central to their understanding of faith. Echoing the words of Jesus, they often say, "If we don't forgive, then we won't be forgiven." Their swift forgiveness of an English neighbor (and his family) who shot ten Amish girls in the West Nickel Mines school in October 2006 illustrates their willingness to respond to injustice with mercy and compassion.

Amish religion often puzzles the modern mind. At first glance, the Amish appear quite religious. Yet a deeper inspection reveals no church buildings, sacred symbols, or formal religious education—even in Amish schools. Religion in the larger American society is usually relegated to an hour or so of services on Sunday morning, but for the Amish, religious meanings permeate all dimensions of life.

Amish spirituality highlights communal expressions of faith. Individuals seldom compose and offer prayers in public. The Lord's Prayer, taught by Jesus in Matthew's gospel, is the primary prayer of Amish faith. It is read at every religious service. Other prayers, from an old Anabaptist prayer book, are also read in church services and family settings. Silent prayers before and after meals illustrate Amish commitments to a quiet faith. Although the Amish value personal Bible reading, they think the Bible should interpret itself. In fact, they discourage small-group Bible studies for fear they might introduce human errors of interpretation, causing endless debates and discord.

Church districts hold services every other Sunday. A group of two hundred or more, including neighbors and relatives from other districts who have an "off Sunday," gather in a home for worship. They may meet in a farmhouse, the basement of a newer home, or a large shop or barn—underscoring the integration of worship with daily life. A modest fellowship meal and informal visiting follow the three-hour service.

The plain and simple, but unwritten, liturgy revolves around a capella singing and two sermons. Without the aid of organs, offerings, candles, crosses, robes, or flowers, the members yield themselves to God in the spirit of humility. The congregation sings from the *Ausbund,* a hymnal of German songs without musical notations that dates back to the sixteenth-century Anabaptists. The tunes, passed across the generations by memory, are sung slowly in unison. The slow, chantlike cadence creates a sixteenth-century mood. A single song may stretch over twenty minutes. Extemporaneous sermons, preached in the German dialect, recount biblical stories as well as lessons from daily life. Preachers exhort members to be obedient to the scriptures and uphold Amish ways.

Amish religion focuses on practicing faith, not repeating creeds or debating doctrine. The Amish way of living needs neither heady talk nor formal theology. Religious understandings are woven into the fabric of living, not written in systematic theologies. Amish spirituality, grounded in *Gelassenheit,* is deeply communal and filled with modesty. In this spirit of humility, the Amish are slow to talk about assurance of salvation. Rather, they speak about having a living hope of eternal life. They do not make bold declarations about their eternal salvation, for they see such pronouncements as presumptuous. They believe that only God can know and make those judgments. "God is the author and finisher of our faith," said an Amish man. "Following Jesus is not about us. It's about him."

From worship to daily life, Amish spirituality emphasizes simplicity. The simple joys of life bring deep satisfaction.

Ordnung

The moral order of Amish life rests on two religious pillars: the teachings of the New Testament and the regulations of the church. The Amish take seriously the biblical teachings on loving enemies, rejecting violence, upholding the sanctity of marriage, and so on. Joining the armed forces or divorcing a spouse would bring excommunication from the church. In addition, the church seeks to apply New Testament principles to daily life through collective regulations known as the *Ordnung,* a German word meaning order and regulations.

A young Amish father explained the importance of communal wisdom this way: "Baseball is not baseball when a batter calls his own balls and strikes. It is not church when each individual decides for himself what should and should not be done."

The *Ordnung* is the communal blueprint for expected behavior, and it regulates private, public, and ceremonial behavior. A cluster of understandings that define Amish ways, the *Ordnung* marks expected Amish behavior, such as wearing a beard, using a carriage, and speaking the dialect. It also specifies taboos: suing someone, wearing jewelry, owning a car, attending college. The understandings, evolving over the years, are updated as the church faces new issues, such as fax machines, computers, cell phones, and working in factories.

The term *world,* in Amish thinking, refers to the outside society, with its values, vices, practices, and institutions. Separation from the world is a key biblical principle that the Amish take seriously. They divide the social world into two pathways: the straight and narrow way to life and the broad, easy road to despair. Amish culture seeks to embody the narrow way of self-denial, whereas the outside social world represents the broad road of vanity and vice. Media reports of greed, fraud, scandal, drugs, violence, divorce, and war confirm, in Amish minds, a world teeming with abomination.

The principle of being separate from the larger culture guides Amish thinking and steers decision-making. Products and practices that might undermine community life, such as cars, cameras, television, computers, or attending high school, are deemed *worldly.* Some new products, such as in-line skates and battery-powered hand tools, are not stigmatized with this label; only those that threaten community values are forbidden. The *Ordnung* translates the religious

The *Ordnung* regulates practices from clothing to technology. These women wear the typical dress of the Lancaster settlement. Adults often use scooters for local travel because car ownership is forbidden.

principle of separation from the world into practical guidelines for living.

The *Ordnung* is passed on by oral tradition. Children also learn the ways of the *Ordnung* by observing adults. The *Ordnung* defines the Amish world—the way things are—in the child's mind. Although ordained leaders review changes to the *Ordnung* in periodic leaders' meetings, the members of each local church district ratify the rules. The leaders interpret the practical application of the *Ordnung*. Thus, dress styles, the use of battery-powered appliances, and power lawn mowers, among other things, vary somewhat from district to district.

Once embedded in the *Ordnung* and established as tradition, the regulations resist change. As new issues face the church, leaders flag those that may disturb community life. Nonthreatening changes, such as gas-powered weed whackers, disposable diapers, and plastic toys, may gradually slip into Amish life. But a battery-powered video camera, which might lead to media entanglements, would surely be taboo. By selectively preserving tradition while also permitting change, the *Ordnung* regulates Amish ways.

~

Religious Rituals and Practices

Religious rituals reflect and articulate the deepest values in Amish culture. They shape Amish identity by reminding members who they are and what they believe.

Baptism

As Anabaptists, the Amish place supreme importance on adult baptism. Those who take the baptismal vow commit themselves to following the ways of Jesus and upholding the *Ordnung* of the church for life. The decision to join the church is the *big* decision for Amish youth. This lifelong promise before God and other members means that they will be accountable to the church for the rest of their lives. If they renege on vows and stray from the church, they will face excommunication and shunning. On the other hand, if they leave the community before baptism, they will not face any formal sanctions, because the Amish respect an individual's voluntary decision regarding church membership.

In the summer before their fall baptism, candidates meet with their district ministers to review the eighteen articles of the 1632 *Dordrecht Confession of Faith.* Young folks are typically baptized between seventeen and twenty-two years of age. Women are often baptized at a younger age than men. The bishop, assisted by the deacon, baptizes candidates by pouring a small amount of water on their heads while they kneel.

Communion

Communion services, held each autumn and spring, frame the religious year. These ritual high points emphasize self-examination and spiritual rejuvenation. Sins are confessed, and members reaffirm their vows to uphold the *Ordnung*. Communion is held when the congregation is "at peace," meaning that all members are in harmony. The eight-hour communion service includes preaching, a light meal during the service, and the commemoration of Christ's death with bread and wine. Pairs of members wash one another's feet as the congregation sings. At the end of the service, members give an alms offering to the deacon. This is the only time that offerings are gathered in Amish services.

Ordination

Ordained officials are called "servants" in the Pennsylvania Dutch dialect. Leaders normally serve for life. They are not paid but may receive occasional love gifts of food. They earn their living in another chosen occupation. Four leaders, holding three roles, typically supervise a church district: a bishop, "servant with full powers"; two ministers, "servants of the book"; and a deacon, "servant to the poor." Guided by the bishop, this leadership team directs the religious life of each district. A bishop typically supervises two church districts. As the spiritual elder, the bishop officiates at baptisms, weddings, communions, funerals, ordinations, and membership meetings.

Ordained leaders are selected by a process known as "the lot." The procedure is based on biblical precedents and employs the mysteries of divine selection. The ritual, held in a home, follows a daylong communion service. Both men and women nominate men, and those who receive three or more votes enter the lot. A slip of paper bearing a Bible verse is placed inside the cover of a hymnbook. The book is then randomly mixed with other hymnbooks to equal the number of candidates, which typically totals five or more. Each candidate selects a book. The officiating bishop says, "Thou Lord, who knows all hearts, show us which of these brethren you have chosen . . ." (Acts 1:24–25). As the books open and the fateful slip of paper appears, the Amish believe the lot falls to the man whom the Lord decrees.

Members' Meetings

The Amish, like other human beings, sometimes forget, rebel, experiment, or stray into deviance. Major transgressions are confessed publicly in occasional

Men provide leadership for church and community life. Women have voices and votes in church meetings, but only men may serve as ordained ministers.

members' meetings after a worship service. Violations of the *Ordnung,* such as using a tractor in the field, posing for a television camera, flying in an airplane, owning a computer, suing in court, joining a political organization, or opening a questionable business, are confessed publicly. Public confession diminishes self-will, reminds members of the supreme value of submission, restores the wayward into the community of faith, and underscores the religious expectations that encircle the community.

Excommunication and Shunning

Headstrong members who spurn the counsel of the congregation and refuse to confess their sins face a temporary probation. If their stubbornness does not mellow into repentance, they face discipline and eventual excommunication. Ex-members also face shunning. Based on biblical teaching, shunning is a form of tough love to remind wayward members that they have broken their baptismal vows. Shunning does not terminate interaction, but it does involve rituals of reminding that restrict some forms of interaction between members and ex-members. For example, members cannot receive a ride in an ex-member's car, eat at the same table, or directly accept financial payments from him or her.

"The purpose of church discipline," said one member, "is to restore the wayward and to discourage members from implicating themselves in the wrongdoing of the wayward." A bishop compared shunning to "the last dose of medicine that you give a sinner. It either works for life or death." Ex-members, even years later, can be restored to membership upon public confession of their sins.

The Architecture of Community Life

Amish society exhibits several distinctive features. It is *local*. Leisure, work, education, play, worship, and friendship revolve around the immediate neighborhood. Many Amish babies enter the world at home or in a local birthing center. Weddings and funerals occur at home. Members may make occasional trips by van or bus to other settlements or even out of state to visit relatives and friends, but for the most part, the Amish world orbits around local turf. From home-canned food to home-cut hair, things are likely to be done near or at home.

Social relationships are *multibonded*. The same people frequently work, play, and worship together. Unlike the fragmented social networks of modern American life, Amish ties have many layers of overlap. Family, friends, and neighbors interact together throughout the life cycle.

Social life is *integrated* into a common fabric. Although some men work on mobile construction crews, most work revolves around the homestead or in a nearby Amish business where children apprentice with their parents. Even in booming small businesses, work remains relatively close to home. Grandparents work and play with their grandchildren in the normal flow of life. All things considered, the segments of social life are woven together more tightly in Amish communities than in the larger society.

Amish society is remarkably *informal*. The tentacles of bureaucracy are sparse. There is no central national office, symbolic figurehead, or institutional headquarters. Apart from schools, committees, and the Pequea Bruderschaft Library, a historical library founded by local Amish, formal institutions do not exist. A loosely organized national steering committee handles government relations for all Amish communities in different states. Committees organize the work of schools, mutual aid, and historical concerns, but bureaucracy, so typical in the modern world, is simply absent.

From egos to organizational units, Amish society reflects the *small-scale* spirit of *Gelassenheit*. Meeting in homes for worship limits the size of congregations. Farms, shops, and schools are relatively small, which increases participation and assures each person a niche in a network of social support.

Informal face-to-face conversations provide the social glue of Amish society. Community decisions are made through discussions in various settings.

Moreover, Amish society is relatively *homogeneous*. The conventional marks of social status—education, income, and occupation—are largely missing. The agrarian heritage placed everyone on common footing. The rise of small industries threatens to disturb the social equality of bygone years, but the range of occupations and social differences remains relatively small. Common dress, horse-and-buggy travel, an eighth-grade education, and equal-size tombstones embody the virtues of social equality.

Mutual aid also distinguishes Amish society. Although the Amish own private property, they, like other Anabaptist communities, have long emphasized mutual aid as a Christian duty in the face of disaster and special needs. Mutual aid extends beyond traditional barn raisings. Many other activities, such as benefit auctions, harvesting, quilting, birthing, marriages, and funerals, require the help of many hands. The habits of care encompass all sorts of needs—drought, disease, injury, death, bankruptcy, as well as medical emergencies. The community springs into action in these moments of despair, articulating the deepest sentiments of Amish life. Discouraging government assistance and commercial insurance, mutual aid reflects Amish self-sufficiency as well as their profound commitment to a humane system of social security at every turn.

~

Family and Children

Amish parents typically raise about seven children, but having ten or more is not uncommon. About 50 percent of the population is under eighteen years of age. A person often has more than seventy-five first cousins, and a typical grandmother may count as many as fifty grandchildren. Members of the extended family frequently live nearby—across the field, down the lane, or beyond the hill. It is impossible to overstate the importance of the family for the socialization of children into Amish culture.

Youth grow up in this thick network of family relations where, as one Amish woman put it, "Everyone knows everyone else's business." One is rarely

Most children have projects that teach them the virtue of work. This boy inspects a pregnant guinea pig. He and his brothers raise guinea pigs for pet shops in urban areas. The sales generate several thousand dollars of income each year.

alone, but is always embedded in a caring community in time of need or disaster. The elderly retire at home, not in geriatric centers away from family. Many grandparents interact with at least some of their grandchildren on a daily basis. From cradle to grave, the community provides a supportive social hammock.

Amish society follows patriarchal patterns. Apart from schoolteachers, who are generally women, men assume the helm of public leadership roles. Women can nominate men to serve in ministerial roles, but they are excluded as candidates. Some women think that because men are in leadership roles, modern equipment is sometimes permitted more readily in barns and shops than in homes. Many women have found new opportunities to develop skills and areas of expertise in the dozens of handicraft businesses that have emerged.

Although husband and wife preside over distinct spheres of domestic life, many tasks are shared. A wife may ask her husband to assist in the garden, and he may ask for her help in the barn or fields. The isolated housewife, trapped in kitchens of industrial societies, is largely absent here. The husband holds spiritual authority in the home, but spouses have considerable freedom within their distinctive spheres. In the words of one Amish man, "The wife is not a servant; she is the queen and the husband is the king." The partnership between husband and wife, as in other societies, varies considerably from family to family and personality to personality.

Childbirth

Upwards of 60 percent of Lancaster's Amish babies greet this world at home under the supervision of non-Amish certified nurse-midwives. Other children in the Lancaster settlement make their debut in birth centers, hospitals, or clinics adjoining a doctor's office. Some mothers prefer a hospital setting for their first birth but then stay home for later ones. Home deliveries not only are cheaper, but also fit the contours of Amish values—local, familial, natural, simple, and self-sufficient.

Certified nurse midwives who deliver babies at home urge Amish parents to take childbirth classes. According to one midwife, most first-time mothers and fathers take the classes. In addition to supervising deliveries, the midwives also offer postpartum care and make home-care visits six weeks after delivery.

Many families share the bounty of their gardens, ovens, and sewing machines with midwives as a special thank-you for home-care services. The tab for a home delivery, including prenatal and postpartum services, is approximately $1,100 per child. Hospital deliveries, by contrast, range from $6,800 for a typical birth to more than $22,000 for a cesarean section. A midwife estimates that the rate of cesarean sections among Amish mothers is 5 percent or less, compared with an average of nearly 25 percent of all births in hospitals. Several physicians provide backup services for midwives and birth centers in the event of complications.

Two relatives often come to assist with household chores at the time of delivery. One stays with the mother and baby for three or four days, and the other runs the household for two weeks. If a mother has teenage daughters, they frequently take over some of the household work.

According to a physician who delivers Amish babies in his clinic, "Amish women are confident about birthing. They know what they're doing. There's always a grandmother nearby to help out." A midwife says, similarly, "They are comfortable with birthing and breast-feeding. They are surrounded by mothers, grandmothers, and older sisters. They see mothering all the time. It's just a normal part of their environment. They are comfortable with labor. I rarely get any requests for pain medication." Virtually all the mothers who have home births and many of those who have hospital births breast-feed their babies.

And what of Amish fathers? Usually nearby, they assist with the birth as needed. "I do have trouble getting fathers to help when it's milking time," says a midwife, "but as a whole, they are attentive, sensitive, and very supportive. The farmers are familiar with animal births, so the whole process doesn't gross them out."

Natural family planning and breast-feeding help space the children. "I don't have many families with less than six children," notes a midwife, "and some have eight to twelve." Although church officials frown on artificial birth control, some couples privately use artificial means to limit family size. Some older women undergo tubal ligations because of medical complications or to terminate childbearing. But as in other areas of Amish life, couples are urged, whenever possible, to yield to the mysteries of Mother Nature.

Two Amish mothers and their babies chat at a public event.

Health Care

Contrary to popular belief, the Amish do use modern medical services—to a certain extent. Lacking physicians within their ranks, they rely on the services of non-Amish dentists, optometrists, and physicians based in health centers, clinics, and hospitals. They cite no biblical injunctions against modern health care or the latest medicines, but they do believe that God is the ultimate healer. Despite the absence of religious taboos on health care, Amish practices do differ from prevailing patterns. Health habits also vary widely from family to family.

Compared with outsiders, the Amish are less likely to seek medical attention for minor aches or illness and more apt to follow folk remedies and drink herbal teas. Although they do not object to surgery or other forms of high-tech treatment, they are less inclined to use heroic lifesaving interventions. They are reticent to quarrel with Mother Nature when their elderly face terminal illness. They are, in short, more willing to yield to the mysteries of divine providence.

In addition to home remedies, members often seek other forms of unorthodox medical treatments. Their search for natural healing often leads them to vitamins, homeopathic remedies, health foods, reflexologists, and chiropractors. One Amish man jokes, "All you would have to do to get Amish people to the moon is to tell them there's a chiropractor there." Some seek the services of special clinics as far away as Mexico. Such clinics may offer treatments, especially for cancer, that are not authorized in the United States. Several Amish entrepreneurs operate health food stores that cater to the Amish as well as to their non-Amish neighbors. Numerous outsiders who market homeopathic treatments and questionable cure-all products seek to entice Amish customers.

Amish health habits are shaped by many cultural factors: conservative rural values, a preference for natural antidotes, a lack of information, a sense of awkwardness in high-tech settings, difficulties accessing health care, as well as a willingness to suffer and lean on the providence of God.

Children may attend Amish schools without immunizations, although the Lancaster community has no religious scruples against vaccinations. Most parents follow the advice of family doctors or nurse-midwives and immunize their children.

An annual quilt auction raises funds to support the work of the Clinic for Special Children, which provides important health services to the Amish community.

Marriages within a stable community and the influx of few converts restrict the genetic pool of Amish society. Marriages sometimes occur between second cousins. Such intermarriage does not necessarily produce medical problems. If unique recessive traits are common in a closed community, however, certain diseases are more likely to occur. On the other hand, a restricted gene pool protects the Lancaster Amish from some hereditary diseases, such as cystic fibrosis. A special type of dwarfism accompanied by other congenital problems occurs at a higher-than-normal rate in the Lancaster settlement. Higher rates of deafness also appear in this community.

In the late 1980s, Dr. O. Holmes Morton identified glutaric aciduria among the Lancaster Amish. Unrecognized and untreatable before, the disease is a biochemical disorder with symptoms similar to cerebral palsy. Approximately 1 in 500 Amish infants inherits the disease. In 1990, Dr. Morton founded the Clinic for Special Children in a cooperative venture with the Amish community. Dr. Morton and his colleagues have identified other inherited diseases and treat newborn children who present symptoms. The clinic, which has boosted health care within the Lancaster Amish community, has also treated many Amish and non-Amish patients far beyond Lancaster County. Moreover, the research conducted by the staff of the clinic also benefits advances in genetic science.

The Amish community has taken a new interest in mental health issues in recent years. An informal network of lay members, known as People Helpers, provide information for families about how to obtain counseling and assistance for members who suffer from some forms of mental illness.

In 2005, an Amish-supervised mental health facility, Green Pastures, was opened on the grounds of Philhaven Psychiatric Hospital, a few miles north of Lancaster County. Supervised by an Amish board of directors, Green Pastures provides short-term care with a living environment that reflects the ethos of Old Order culture—no televisions, radios, or computers. Professionally trained and certified social workers and psychiatrists serve the patients. Green Pastures reflects a new interest and commitment of Lancaster's Amish to serve the mental health needs of their people.

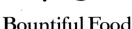

Bountiful Food

The bounty on Amish tables flows from a Pennsylvania Dutch culinary tradition shared with other groups in southeastern Pennsylvania. Food preferences among Lancaster's Amish vary by family and also somewhat between farm and nonfarm households. Although food lies beyond the reach of religious regulations, a traditional menu is served at meals following church services, weddings, and funerals.

Breakfast fare for many families may include eggs, fried potatoes, toast, and commercial cereals such as Corn Flakes and Cheerios. Typical breakfast foods also include shoofly pie, sometimes dipped in or covered with coffee or milk; stewed crackers in warm milk; oatmeal, rolled or instant; mush made from cornmeal; and sausage. Puddings and scrapple are also breakfast favorites. The puddings consist of ground liver, heart, and kidneys from pork and beef. These basic ingredients are combined with flour and cornmeal to produce scrapple. The particular mix of breakfast menu foods on an Amish table varies by season and family preference.

For farm families, the midday dinner is usually the largest meal of the day. Noontime dinners and evening suppers often include beef or chicken dishes and vegetables in season—peas, corn, green beans, lima beans, or carrots—from the family garden. Mashed potatoes covered with beef gravy, noodles with brown butter, chicken pot pie, and sauerkraut are regional favorites. Side dishes and desserts may include applesauce, cornstarch pudding, tapioca, or fruit pies in season—apple, rhubarb, pumpkin—as well as schnitz pies made from dried apples.

Potato soup, vegetable soup, and chicken-corn-noodle soup are commonplace. In summer months, cold fruit soups, consisting of strawberries, raspberries, or blueberries added to milk and bread cubes, appear on Amish tables. Meadow tea, homemade root beer, and instant drink mixes are used in the summer. Home-canned grape juice is a wintertime favorite.

Food preservation and preparation for large families and sizable gatherings are enormous undertakings. Families hosting church services in their homes often bake three dozen pies for the noontime meal following the gathering. Quantities of canned food vary by family size and preference. It is not uncom-

Barbecued chicken is a favorite food. Young men prepare the chicken in the background. Mobile barbecue units like this one are manufactured in Amish shops.

mon for a family with six children to can 150 quarts of applesauce, 100 quarts of peaches, 60 quarts of pears, 50 quarts of grape juice, and 50 quarts of pizza sauce in one growing season. Many other fruits, vegetables, and meats are also preserved in jars.

Amish diets are still anchored in family gardens, but changes are afoot. An increasing proportion of food is purchased from stores, sometimes operated by the Amish. One Amish woman estimates that only half of Amish families bake their own bread. The growing use of instant puddings, instant drinks, snack foods, and canned soups not only signal a tilt toward commercial food, but reflect growing time constraints as well. The use of commercial food rises as families leave the farm, and especially as women enter entrepreneurial roles. There are also economic considerations. A farmer's wife notes that "gardens are hardly worth the effort when you can buy canned fruits and vegetables in bulk so cheap." This also applies to butchering, which one Amish man called "a lost art."

Nearby fast-food restaurants and convenience stores also provide a growing source of food for some Amish. Indeed, some people who work away from home eat a few of their meals at restaurants. Church leaders discourage families from eating out on a regular basis, however. Also of interest is the arrival of ethnic foods. Homemade pizza is a favorite of many Lancaster Amish families. Pizza sauce made from homegrown tomatoes is canned in large quantities. Lasagna, stromboli, and even taco salads and nacho chips are found on some Amish tables.

Social Gatherings and Holidays

A variety of social gatherings bring Amish community members together for times of fellowship and fun. Young people gather in homes for Sunday evening singings. Married couples sometimes meet with old friends to sing for shut-ins and elderly members in their homes. Frolics blend work and play together. Parents gather for preschool frolics in order to ready schools for September classes. End-of-school picnics bring parents and students together for afternoons of food and games.

Quilting bees, barn raisings, and benefit auctions mix goodwill, levity, and hard work for young and old alike. Other occasions of collective work, such as cleaning up after a fire, plowing for an ill neighbor, gardening for a sick mother, or filling a silo, involve neighbors and extended families in episodes of charity, sweat, and fun. Adult sisters, sometimes numbering as many as five or six, gather for a "sisters' day," which blends laughter with cleaning, quilting, canning, or gardening in one of their homes.

Public auctions of farm equipment in February and March attract large crowds on a homestead. Besides opportunities to bid on equipment, these daylong auctions offer ample time for socializing and friendly fun. Games of cornerball in a nearby field or barnyard often compete with the drama of the auction. Household auctions and horse sales provide other favorite times to socialize.

Family gatherings during religious holidays as well as summer family reunions rejuvenate familial networks. Single women sometimes gather at a cabin or home for a weekend of fun and leisure. Members of the Lancaster settlement also attend nationwide annual meetings of persons with specialized interests—harnessmakers, cabinetmakers, metal workers, accountants, businesswomen, teachers, and families with disabled members.

The Amish holiday calendar underscores the community's separation from the larger world. As conscientious objectors, the Amish have little enthusiasm for patriotic days with a military flair. Memorial Day, Veterans Day, and the Fourth of July are barely noticed. Even Labor Day stirs little interest. The witches and goblins of Halloween feel foreign to Amish spirits. Pumpkins without cut faces are displayed by some families, but Halloween parties are never held.

Amish holidays preserve the rhythm of the seasons and traditional religious celebrations. These furloughs from work imbue a religious tone to the Amish year. A day for prayer and fasting precedes each communion service in the fall and spring. A flurry of fall weddings, held on Tuesdays and Thursdays, provide ample "holidays" for visiting and celebrating. Those without a wedding to attend on Thanksgiving Day celebrate the day with turkey dinners and family gatherings. New Year's Day is a quiet time for family gatherings, not intoxicating parties and marathon football games. A second day for socializing is added to Christmas, Easter, and Pentecost. The actual holiday is a sacred time filled with quiet family activities. The following day—second Christmas, Easter Monday, and Pentecost Monday—provides time for recreation, visiting, and sometimes shopping. Ascension Day, prior to Pentecost, is a holiday for visiting, fishing, and other forms of recreation. Often friends from *Rumspringa* days visit together on these springtime holidays. "More visiting takes place on these springtime holidays," says one Amish man, "than at any other time."

Christmas and Easter festivities are relatively free from commercial trappings. Families exchange Christmas cards and gifts. Some presents are homemade crafts and practical gifts, but increasingly many are store-bought. Homes are decorated with greens, but Christmas trees, stockings, special lights, Santa Claus, and mistletoe are missing. Although eggs are sometimes painted and children may be given a basket of candy, Easter bunnies rarely, if ever, visit Amish homes. The sacred holidays revolve around religious customs and family gatherings rather than commercial trinkets and the sounds of worldly hubbub.

Homemade ice cream is a favorite food at social gatherings. This man uses a minia-ture steam engine to turn a large ice cream freezer *(far right, hidden from view).*

Birthdays are celebrated at home and school in quiet but pleasant ways—with cakes and gifts, but not large-scale parties filled with clowns, balloons, and noisemakers. Parents often share a special snack of cake and ice cream, cookies or Popsicles with school friends to honor a child's birthday. Holiday festivities in the Amish world reaffirm religious roots, strengthen family ties, and underscore the lines of separation from the larger culture.

Leisure

Leisure and pleasure have historically been regarded with suspicion in Amish culture. Idleness is viewed as the devil's workshop. But the recent rise of small industries has brought additional cash to support more recreational activities. Says one Amish entrepreneur, "We're business people now, not just backwoods farmers, and sometimes we just need to get away from things."

For the most part, the new recreational ventures remain entrenched in Amish values. The activities are group oriented, and they tilt more toward nature and travel than commercial entertainment. For example, camping in meadows

Volleyball is a favorite leisure activity, especially among young people.

or woodlots is very popular. The Lancaster Amish rarely take "vacations," but they do take "trips" to Amish settlements in other states by chartered bus or van. These may include side trips to scenic sites, such as the Skyline Drive in the Shenandoah Valley of Virginia or Niagara Falls. Some patients seeking medical care in Mexico may visit natural sites of beauty in the U.S. Southwest. Groups often travel to other settlements for reunions, special gatherings, or historical tours, or visit state parks or city zoos. Some people join commercial chartered bus trips to historical sites. Buses and vans also transport volunteer crews to disaster areas, where they blend leisure with goodwill as they clean up and rebuild after floods, tornadoes, or hurricanes.

Among youth, seasonal athletics, such as softball, sledding, skating, hockey, snow and water skiing, and swimming, are common. Volleyball is a widespread favorite. Some youth play tennis and racquetball. Most enjoy swimming in farm ponds and nearby streams, but other teens travel to the beach for a summer splash.

Fishing and game hunting are favorite sports. Some Amish men own hunting cabins in other counties of Pennsylvania, where they hunt white-tailed deer and enjoy a reprieve from home. Deep-sea-fishing trips are common summertime jaunts for men. Other families prefer fishing in local streams or canoeing. Pitching quoits is common at family reunions and picnics. Some youth, and occasionally adults, head west for big-game hunting, snowmobiling, or snow skiing.

Older couples sometimes travel to Florida for several weeks over the winter and live in an Amish retirement village near Sarasota that is populated by Amish "snowbirds" from several states. Some joke that Sarasota is "the spot for newlyweds, nearly deads, and punkheads."

Although Amish folks travel for leisure by train or bus, chartered vans are by far the most popular mode. By traveling together with family, friends, and extended kin, these mobile groups enjoy the laughter and chatter that bond and build community life.

~

Schools and Teachers

Amish children attended one-room rural public schools in the first half of the twentieth century. Under local control, these schools posed little threat to Amish values. But the massive consolidation of public schools in the early 1950s sparked clashes between the Amish and state officials. After legal skirmishes in several states, the U.S. Supreme Court gave its blessing to the eight-grade Amish school system in 1972, permitting Amish youth to stop formal schooling at the age of fourteen.

Today thirty to thirty-five "scholars," as the Amish call schoolchildren, attend each of the nearly 200 Amish one-room schools in the Lancaster settlement. Scripture reading and recitation of the Lord's Prayer open each day, but religion is not formally taught in the school. The curriculum includes reading, arithmetic, spelling, grammar, penmanship, history, and some geography. Classes are conducted in English, but German is part of the curriculum. Science and sex education are missing, as are many other typical trappings of public schools—sports, dances, cafeterias, clubs, bands, choruses, computers, television, teacher strikes, guidance counselors, principals, and college recruiters.

A local board of three to five fathers organizes the school, hires a teacher, approves the curriculum, oversees the budget, and supervises maintenance. Amish teachers, trained in Amish schools, are not certified by state officials. They are the brightest and best of Amish scholars who return to the classroom to teach, often in their late teens and early twenties. Amish school directors select them for their ability to teach, their commitment to Amish values, and their availability. Amish teachers are frequently single women who terminate their teaching when they marry. Without the benefit of high school or college diplomas or any formal training, they manage nearly thirty pupils across eight grades. Periodic meetings with other teachers, a monthly teachers' magazine, and ample common sense prepare them for the task.

On the last day of school, a first-grader walks to school early. She bursts into the classroom with a smile and runs up to her teacher. "These are for you," she says, beaming as she hands her a bouquet of daffodils. "I picked them down by the stream." Other pupils bring their own last-day gifts: needlework, baked goods, crafts, and woodwork. These fruits of love flow from youthful hearts on a mid-May morning. "I'm not in this for the money," says one teacher. "There are deeper rewards—smiles of pleasure at a parents' program, an evening with a family, a birthday celebration, and an invitation to a wedding. These are the things that make it worthwhile."

With three or four pupils per grade, teachers often instruct two grades at a time. Classrooms exhibit a distinct sense of order amid a beehive of activity. Hands raise to ask permission to use the outhouse, get a library book, or clarify instructions as the teacher moves from grade to grade every ten or fifteen minutes.

The ethos of the classroom accents cooperative activity, obedience, respect, diligence, kindness, and the natural world. Little attention is given to inde-

Nearly 200 one-room schools are scattered across the Lancaster Amish settlement.

pendent thinking and critical analysis, the esteemed values of public education. Despite the emphasis on order, playful pranks and giggles are commonplace. Schoolyard play in daily recesses often involves softball or various homespun games.

Students receive a remarkable amount of personal attention, despite the teacher's responsibility for eight grades. Teachers know parents personally as well as the special circumstances surrounding each child. Children in some cases have the same teacher for all eight grades. Indeed, all the children from a family may have the same teacher.

Amish schools promote practical skills to prepare their graduates for success in Amish society. Some testing indicates that Amish pupils compare favorably with rural peers in public schools on standardized tests of basic skills. Although different from public schools, these small schools prepare Amish children for meaningful lives in Amish society by teaching cooperation, responsibility, hard work, and basic skills for living. These one-room schools play a critical role in preserving Amish culture. They reinforce Amish values and also shield pupils from contaminating ideas. Amish schools harbor the young within the confines of an Amish world as they step toward adulthood.

Rumspringa

In recent years, *Rumspringa* has become a recognized word in the larger society because of the media spotlight on Amish teenagers in television programs such as *Amish in the City.* The late-teenage years are an ambiguous stage in Amish life. Like other young people, Amish teens swing between the innocence of childhood and the responsibilities of adulthood. Amish youth, however, bypass high school and college and spend little time "finding themselves" as they move directly from adolescence to adulthood. When they turn sixteen years of age, Amish youth begin going out with their peers on weekends. This period of *Rumspringa,* or "running around," is the time when many of them begin courtship. This stage of Amish life ends at marriage.

Teens in the Lancaster area join one of two dozen youth groups that criss-cross the settlement. Adult chaperones give oversight to more than half of the groups, but the others determine their own activities. Each group of 100 to 200 members has a name, such as Bluebirds, Drifters, or Shotguns, and gathers for supper and singing at a member's home on Sunday evenings. They play volley-ball in seasonable weather and toss darts or compete at table tennis in winter months. Groups also play softball and go skating and hiking.

Some of the unchaperoned groups occasionally become rebellious and sometimes snub Amish values. Members of a few of these groups own cars, attend movies, venture into the city to socialize in bars, or go to the beach for a weekend fling. Some of the groups may rent buildings where they meet and

Courtship typically begins during *Rumspringa.*

sometimes host parties. Such activities embarrass church leaders and pain the hearts of parents. In 1998, two unbaptized Amish youths were arrested for buying cocaine from members of the Pagans Motorcycle Club and reselling it to their Amish friends. The sensational story stirred a feeding frenzy among news media around the world. Amish parents and elders were embarrassed by the rare incident and worked hard to educate other Amish young people about the dangers of drugs. Despite such flirtations with worldliness, nine out of ten youths eventually join the church.

At baptism, young adults declare their Christian faith and promise to be faithful members of the church for the rest of their lives. Those who break their baptismal vows face excommunication and shunning. Young people who choose not to be baptized gradually drift away from the community, but they are welcome to continue socializing with their families without the stigma of shunning.

The practice of sowing wild oats during *Rumspringa* gives youth the impression that church membership is a choice—and to some extent, it is. Some seek other paths, but for the most part, the forces of Amish life funnel them toward baptism. Beyond the web of family, friends, school, and romantic ties, economic incentives also pull young people homeward. The freedom of the teenage years creates the perception of choice, and that perception encourages adults to uphold the *Ordnung* in later life. After all, they had a chance to explore the outside world and count the cost of membership before joining the church. Such thinking bolsters adult commitment to the church.

Weddings

The wedding season is a festive time. The Lancaster community typically hosts about 150 weddings on Tuesdays and Thursdays after the harvest season, from late October through early December and sometimes into January. Fifteen weddings may be scattered across the settlement on the same day. Typically staged at the home of the bride, these joyous events involve upward of 350 guests, and include a three-hour religious service followed by two meals, singing, snacks, and festivities.

A wedding is typically held at the home of the bride. The building on the right was renovated to accommodate some 300 guests for this wedding.

Young persons typically marry in their early twenties. Only baptized members of the church may marry. Young men begin growing a beard, the functional equivalent of a wedding ring, soon after their marriage. The church does not arrange mates, but it does place its blessing on the pair through an old ritual. Before the wedding, the groom takes a letter signed by church elders to the bride's deacon testifying to the groom's good standing in his home district. The bride's deacon then meets with her to verify the marriage plans.

The wedding day is an enormous undertaking for the bride's family, as well as for relatives and friends who assist with preparations. Efforts to clean up the property, paint rooms, fix furniture, pull weeds, and pave driveways, among other things, begin weeks in advance. The logistics of preparing two meals as well as snacks for several hundred guests are taxing.

The three-hour service, without flowers, rings, solos, or instrumental music, is similar to an Amish worship service. The wedding includes congregational singing, prayers, wedding vows, and two sermons. Four single friends, usually siblings or relatives, serve the bride and groom as attendants; however, no one is designated maid of honor or best man. Amish brides typically make their own wedding dresses from blue or purple material crafted in traditional styles. The bride wears a white cap and an apron over her dress. In addition to the groom's new but customary black coat and vest, he and his attendants often wear small black bow ties.

The noontime wedding menu features chicken roast, which is chicken mixed with bread filling and served with mashed potatoes, gravy, creamed celery, pepper cabbage, and other items. Desserts include pears, peaches, and puddings, plus dozens of pies and hundreds of cookies and doughnuts.

Games, snacks, and singing follow the noon meal, which involves several seatings. Each boy chooses a girl for the afternoon singing. Following the evening meal, another, more lively singing takes place in which the bride pairs off unmarried young people who are not dating. Dating couples pair off together, arousing considerable interest, because for some this may be their first appearance as a couple. Festivities may continue until nearly midnight as guests gradually leave. Some guests, invited to several weddings on the same day, may rotate among them.

Newly married couples usually set up housekeeping in the spring after their wedding. Until then, the groom may live at the bride's home or continue to live with his parents. In lieu of a traditional honeymoon, couples visit relatives on weekends during the winter months. Several newlywed couples may make visiting rounds together, sometimes staying overnight at the homes of close relatives. During this time of visitation, family and friends present gifts to the newlyweds, adding to the bride's dowry, which often consists of some furniture.

Stewards of the Soil

Amish life is rooted in the soil. Ever since European persecution pushed them into rural areas, the Amish have been tillers of the soil—and good ones, too. The land has nurtured their common life and robust families. "It's been a long-standing tradition," says one leader, "that Amish families live on the farm, attached closely to the soil, and a good father provides a farm for his boys." But these long-standing customs are under assault from suburban sprawl and shopping malls in Lancaster County. Thousands of acres of farmland are covered with asphalt and new housing developments every year. As urbanization devours prime farmland, land prices soar. Farmland in the heart of Lancaster's Amish settlement sells for $15,000 an acre or higher, making it impossible for young couples to buy land, equipment, and livestock, pay off their debts, and earn a living by farming.

The shrinking availability of farmland has forced a crisis in the Amish soul. The community has coped with the crisis in several ways. Farms have been sub-divided into smaller sections for intensive cropping and larger concentrations of livestock. New forms of farming include raising produce to sell at wholesale auctions and urban farmers markets. Some farmers have turned to organic veg-etables, milk, and eggs, which bring higher prices, and others raise pets to sell to pet stores. To escape the urban encroachment, some families have migrated to the rural backwaters of other states, where they can purchase cheaper land. Other families continue to live on farms, which they consider the best place to raise a family, but rent out their land to non-Amish tractor farmers.

About 30 percent of Lancaster's Amish families still earn their living by till-ing the soil. The primary income for traditional farmers is milk. To qualify for the best milk prices, Amish farmers chill their milk in bulk tanks with refriger-ation units powered by diesel engines instead of public electricity. They also use automatic vacuum milkers to milk cows. Up-to-date veterinary services, vacci-nations, medications, and commercial feed supplements enhance the produc-tivity of Amish dairies. Agricultural consultants advise Amish farmers on the use of fertilizers, pesticides, and herbicides.

Although modern in many appearances, Amish farms differ from non-Amish operations in several ways. Trying to cap the size of dairy herds in order to keep them family operations, the *Ordnung* prohibits milking parlors, silo

A young teenager, with assistance from her father and siblings, takes the lead role in managing the morning and evening milking of some thirty Holstein cows.

unloaders, automatic gutter cleaners, and glass pipelines for pumping milk from cows to chilling tanks. These measures keep Amish herds much smaller than non-Amish ones. Feed and manure handling is often powered by hydraulic or air-driven pumps and elevators.

Dairy farming leans heavily on alfalfa and corn crops for feed. Cut four times throughout the summer, alfalfa is baled into hay for winter feeding. Fields of green corn, stalks and all, are chopped and blown into tall silos. Dried ear corn, picked in the fall, is shelled and ground for cattle feed. Leftover corn fodder is often baled for bedding.

Despite the automation, a sixty-acre dairy farm with forty cows, with an assortment of thirty calves and heifers, as well as ten mules and horses, entails endless work. Nearly 400 tons of green corn silage are cut in late August, hauled to the barn, and blown into silos for winter feeding. Moreover, about 100 tons of hay are baled in dusty fields and transported to the barn for storage. Approximately 90 tons of ear corn are harvested for storage. Roughly 2 tons of feed are distributed to livestock each day in the winter. Plus, hundreds of tons of manure are hauled and spread on the fields as fertilizer. All of this means that, despite the automation, farm work remains hard and dirty.

To help stem the tide of urban development, many Amish landowners have cooperated with land preservation efforts in Lancaster County. They are paid a per-acre fee if they agree to legally preserve their land for farming. Since 1991, about 135 Amish farms, totaling nearly 9,000 acres, have been protected from development. These efforts have guaranteed that at least some Amish farms will be preserved for future generations.

A Mini Industrial Revolution

Lancaster's Amish have steadfastly spurned factory work, fearing that it would fragment families and expose adults to cultural vices. Moreover, they believe that "lunch-pail work" would untie the knot of communal dependency if members received insurance and other fringe benefits that flow from factory work. Squeezed off the land, deploring the factory, yet wanting to remain near ancestral homesteads, Amish leaders made a compromise. They would leave the land, but they would not trudge off to factories. Instead, they would create their own factories—small cottage industries anchored in Amish values.

The rise of small industries marks a historic turn in the life of Lancaster's Amish community. Mushrooming since the 1980s, these new enterprises have reshaped the Amish landscape. Joking about the array of new jobs, an old sage chimes, "About the only thing we don't have now is an undertaker." Though not quite true, his quip illustrates the booming growth of Amish businesses. Retail shops sell dry goods, furniture, shoes, and bulk foods. Church members now work as carpenters, plumbers, painters, and self-trained accountants. Professionals such as lawyers, physicians, and veterinarians are missing from Amish ranks.

The new industries come in three forms. Home-based operations, located on farms or adjacent to homes, employ a few family members and neighbors. Bakeshops, craft shops, hardware stores, health-food stores, greenhouses, quilt shops, flower shops, and repair shops of all sorts illustrate some of the hundreds of home-based operations. Work in these settings revolves around the family. "What we're trying to do," says one proprietor, "is to keep the family together." A growing number of these small cottage industries cater to tourists, but many serve the needs of Amish and non-Amish neighbors alike.

Larger shops and manufacturing concerns are housed in newly constructed buildings on the edges of farms or on commercial plots. These shops, typically with fifteen or fewer employees, manufacture farm machinery, hydraulic equipment, storage barns, furniture, and cabinetry. Metal fabrication shops thrive on subcontracts with other manufacturers. These larger industries are efficient and profitable. Low overhead, minimal advertising, austere management, modest wages, quality workmanship, and sheer hard work grant many shops a competitive edge in the marketplace.

Mobile work crews constitute a third type of industry. Amish construction groups travel to building sites in Lancaster County and surrounding areas. Dozens of mobile crews have profited from the building boom in Lancaster County. The construction crews travel in hired vehicles and use the latest tools powered by portable generators or on-site electricity. Operating stands at farmers markets is another form of mobile work. Several hundred Amish people operate or tend stands several days a week at markets in south central Pennsylvania, New Jersey, Delaware, and Maryland.

These new industries bear the imprint of Amish culture in several ways. They are, first of all, small. Church leaders fear that businesses with dozens of employees will bring pride, worldliness, excessive power, and publicity—the evil trappings of large-scale operations. A smaller scale offers flexible work schedules to accommodate community activities, such as funerals, weddings, and special holidays. Small-scale operations harbor the dignity of work and pride in craftsmanship. Without professional training, the Amish nevertheless act as professionals because they control the terms and conditions of their work. One of the remarkable signs of success is the low failure rate of new Amish businesses. Less than 5 percent fail, whereas the national average for small-business failures exceeds 65 percent.

This mini industrial revolution is the largest and most significant social change since the Amish arrived in Lancaster County in the 1700s. In the long run, the rise of business will disturb the social equality of Amish life by encouraging a three-tier society of farmers, entrepreneurs, and day laborers. Will prosperous shop owners turn their profits back to the community or spend them on upscale lifestyles? "And even if they turn their profits back to the community," asks one Amish man, "will their influence bolster their egos in unhealthy ways?" Parents worry that youth, working a forty-hour week with cash in their pockets, will snub the traditional Amish values of simplicity and frugality. The new industries increase contact with the outside world, and such exchanges, over the generations, will surely prompt more changes in Amish life.

Boys play on a forklift at a public auction. The shift to nonfarm occupations exposes young children to many new forms of technology.

Women Entrepreneurs

The mini industrial revolution has opened new occupational doors for Amish women. Traditionally tied to farm and homestead, some women are now in entrepreneurial roles. Single women have long worked as domestics and clerks in a variety of non-Amish settings. The emergence of Amish businesswomen, however, is a new turn. Untouched by the winds of feminism, women entrepreneurs are flourishing for a variety of reasons.

The declining availability of farmland presses some families to search for new ways of earning a living. Flocks of tourists, hungry for Amish crafts, provide an easy and ready market for traditional handicrafts such as quilts. The rise of cottage industries has also spurred the creative development of new crafts.

Church leaders typically are not involved in a woman's decision to open a business. They do not discourage women from entering business, but they do discourage them from working away from home if they have young children. Some of the new businesswomen are single, but others are grandmothers. Still others are mothers of young families. In all of these cases, women continue to do household duties, often assisted by their children.

Amish women operate a variety of businesses, mostly from their homes or adjacent offices. Many tend small roadside stands on a seasonal basis in tandem with household activities. They sell garden produce, crafts, canned fruits, jellies, and baked goods. Others manage permanent enterprises, such as clothing stores, food stores, bakeshops, greenhouses, flower shops, and tailor shops. Some operate or tend stands at farmers markets in metropolitan areas several hours away from Lancaster County. One woman hosts a bed-and-breakfast operation. Another is self-employed as an artist. And quiltmaking, of course, is big business. Quilting operations are sometimes divided into production stages at different locations. Entrepreneurs purchase quilts in various stages of completion from Amish women living in other counties and even out of state. The women who manage these operations supervise the final quilting and sell the quilts to wholesale dealers or place them on the retail market. Some Amish women find employment as hostesses, consultants, or distributors for home-based direct marketing parties selling Tupperware, Pampered Chef, and Princess House, to name the most common ones.

These young women learn the skills of entrepreneurship by selling sodas at public events.

Cottage industries typically involve the preparation and sale of products long associated with female roles, such as baked goods, garden produce, quilts, health foods, and clothing. These commercial ventures embrace the values of the Amish moral order: small, family-held, and family-operated. It would be unthinkable, for example, for a woman to sell cosmetics, operate a video store, or open a styling salon.

Amish businesswomen, who have long deferred to their husbands to handle queries from outsiders, now freely interact with non-Amish suppliers, retailers, and customers. The entrepreneurs are developing commercial skills in marketing, accounting, labor relations, and management. They also enjoy a stream of income separate from their husbands—independence unheard of in former days. These dual-income arrangements and the rise of women in business will surely alter gender roles in years to come.

The Motor Vehicle Maze

Amish use of automobiles is perplexing. They are permitted to ride in motor vehicles but not to own or drive them. This baffling practice appears inconsistent to some outsiders, but it makes sense within the scope of Amish history.

Gaining popularity in the second decade of the twentieth century, automobiles freed people to travel independently, whenever and wherever they pleased. The car became the symbol of American independence as it liberated people from train and trolley schedules and broke the confines of geography and the provincialism of rural life.

This van pulls a trailer filled with baked goods for a market stand operated by these women. Many Amish businesses hire taxis provided by outsiders on a daily basis.

For a rural people who strove to remain separate from the world, however, this new invention spelled trouble. Automatic mobility was a menace to a community that wanted to stay together and hoped to avoid city life. The car collided with the very core of Amish culture. It symbolized the delights of modernity—freedom, acceleration, power, mobility, autonomy, and individualism. The automobile was the charm of an individuated, mobile society, but not of a stable rural people who cherished community.

If given keys to a car, individuals might drive away to urban worlds of vice and pleasure. Church members would soon be out of sight, free-floating, and independent. Individuals might also use cars to flaunt their status and disrupt the equality of Amish life. And cars would surely accelerate the pace of life. Amish leaders feared that the car would unravel social ties in the local church district and, in short, pull the community apart.

Sensing the danger, church leaders placed a taboo on car *ownership* about 1915. *Use* of motor vehicles emerged slowly in the first half of the twentieth century, as members sometimes rode in the cars of their non-Amish neighbors. As the Amish settlement expanded, it became difficult to travel to outlying areas by horse and carriage in a single day. So gradually the use of motor vehicles for business, emergencies, and social visits began to rise.

Some non-Amish people began offering the Amish taxi service for pay on a regular basis after 1950. Many non-Amish drivers now earn full or supplemental incomes by providing taxi service in their private vehicles for Amish to travel in the Lancaster area, as well as to distant sites. Families and friends often travel together in hired vans to funerals, weddings, and other social gatherings beyond the reach of horse-and-buggy transportation.

The rise of flourishing Amish industries accelerated the use of motor vehicles. Amish businesses frequently hire vehicles to transport supplies and deliver products. Mobile carpentry crews travel to construction sites by hired van and truck. Some businesses have a non-Amish employee who provides a vehicle for company use.

The firm line between the *use* and *ownership* of motor vehicles illustrates a cultural compromise between modernity and tradition. This practical solution keeps the car at bay, all the while using it to enhance community and bolster commerce. Restricted mobility keeps families together, holds work close to home, and preserves social interaction in local districts. Controlled use of the car keeps faith with Amish tradition while also giving some freedom to maneuver in the larger society.

Tractors and Farm Machinery

Tractors present another riddle of Amish life. They are standard equipment on farms, but they rarely venture into fields. Why are tractors used at barns but not in fields? This riddle, like many others, is rooted in history. Tractors became available to American farmers in the early 1920s, at a time when Amish leaders had already banned the car. Elders worried that farmers might drive tractors to town for supplies or even groceries. Over time, such habits would surely lead to use of the car.

But there were other reasons to worry about tractors working in Amish fields. First, they would steal work from Amish boys. Unlike modern folks, who are eager to save labor at every turn, the Amish welcome work as a wholesome way of keeping families together. Tethering tractors to the barn preserved field work for Amish lads and kept them out of factory work, which might pull families apart. Furthermore, the use of horses bridles farming operations, keeping them small enough to be managed by one family. Moreover, self-propelled harvesting equipment would soon tag along with tractors. In short, the Amish feared that tractors and self-propelled equipment would wreak havoc on family life and lead to large, corporate-style farms.

But why permit tractors at the barn? Since the 1880s, Amish farmers had used steam engines to power threshing machines. Small internal-combustion engines also powered wood saws, feed grinders, water pumps, and washing machines. Thus when elders restricted tractors to barn use, they were merely freezing history—using engines for extra power around the barn as they had done in the past.

Tractors at Amish barns power feed grinders, spin ventilating fans, run manure pumps, operate hydraulic systems, and blow silage to the top of steep silos. This arrangement serves the Amish well. Tied to the barn, tractors bring extra torque to dairy operations without threatening family or community life. Most important, the Amish retain the horse as a compelling symbol of their identity.

Instead of tractors, horses and mules pull modern machinery across Amish fields. This surprising marriage appears silly at first glance. When the Amish rejected tractors for field work, horse-drawn implements were still easy to

Mules pull a state-of-the-art corn planter. A gasoline engine powers a vacuum pump that drops seeds exactly ten inches apart on each row.

obtain. As non-Amish farmers replaced their horses with tractors, the availability of horse-drawn equipment naturally dwindled. The Amish faced several options: manufacture their own horse-drawn implements, convert tractor implements for horse use, or begin using tractors in the field. The taboo on tractors in the field held firm.

Amish shops began manufacturing their own horse-drawn equipment—plows, wagons, manure spreaders, sprayers, and corn planters. Most Amish farmers also began adopting modern tractor equipment so that it could be pulled by horses. In the 1950s, several Amish farmers bought mechanical hay balers and adapted them to be pulled by horses. By mounting an engine on the baler for power and supporting its weight on a forecart with a seat and wheels, the baler could be pulled by horses. This curious blend of tradition and progress became a turning point in Amish farming. Soon other implements powered by engines and towed by mules or horses spiked the productivity of farming operations.

Over the years, more machinery designed for tractors was adapted for horse use by Amish mechanics. Gasoline engines appeared on grass mowers, corn pickers, roto beaters, and sprayers, among other implements. A good compromise, this keeps the horse in the field and the family on the farm. It slows things down but also taps new power sources to harvest robust crops and boost productivity. Like other riddles of technology, this one strikes a delicate balance between tradition and technological progress.

~

"Amish Electricity"

Electrical appliances, such as clothes dryers, hair dryers, air conditioners, dishwashers, VCRs, and TVs, are conspicuously missing from Amish homes, but electricity is used in other ways. Flashing red lights on buggies warn approaching traffic. Electric fences encircle cattle pastures. The elderly sometimes read by battery-powered lamps. Flashlights sit on household shelves. Carpentry crews use electrical power saws, and welding machines abound on Amish farms. What sort of logic underlies this maze of electrical use?

The Amish forbade the use of public electricity as power lines were creeping into rural areas in the early 1920s. For folks who were trying to insulate themselves from the larger society and assert their self-sufficiency, it made little sense to become hooked onto the power grid of the outside world.

The Amish had always used batteries to start motors and power flashlights, and they simply continued to use batteries in old and new ways. As electricity permeated the larger society, a distinction gelled in the Amish mind between the 12-volt (DC) current stored in batteries and the 110-volt (AC) current tapped from public lines. The Amish taboo on 110-volt current eliminated debate over all the new electrical gadgets that flooded American homes. As one Amish man notes, "It's not so much electricity that we're against, it's all the things that come with it—all the modern appliances, televisions, and computers. If we get electric lights, then where will we stop?"

Elders eventually permitted electric welders in Amish machine shops and the use of electric power tools by carpenters at construction sites. In addition, small inverters are allowed to convert 12-volt current from batteries into 110-volt "homemade" electricity to operate cash registers, calculators, digital scales, and copiers. Twelve-volt motors operate a variety of small machines in Amish farms and shops. Some homes also use batteries to operate appliances such as cake mixers.

This large wood sander is operated by air and hydraulic power instead of electricity. Propane gas fuel is used to light the shop.

The taboo on 110-volt electricity, however, sharply crimped the productivity of Amish businesses. Could shops be powered by nonelectric sources of energy? The question became urgent with the rise of small industries in the 1970s.

Amish mechanics soon discovered that hydraulic or air motors could operate large equipment. Hydraulic and air pumps, powered by diesel engines, force oil or air through hoses to motors that spin grinders, saws, and other machines. Several Amish shops specialize in converting equipment from electrical power to air and hydraulic power. An unwritten rule quickly emerged: "If you can do it with air or oil, you may do it." Touting the success of "Amish electricity," one shop owner chortles, "We can do anything with air and hydraulic that you can do with electricity!" The productivity of Amish shops has soared with the aid of lathes, drills, sanders, and metal presses, to name only a few of the many machines that run on "Amish electricity."

Diesel engines also provide power for a variety of purposes on Amish farms. Farmers tap air and hydraulic power to turn fans, power elevators, operate feeders, and pump water. Air and hydraulic pumps, powered by diesel engines, ease work in many Amish households as well. Washing machines, sewing machines, ice cream freezers, and food processors sometimes run on "Amish electricity."

Propane gas is used to power refrigerators, stoves, hot-water heaters, and gas lanterns in Amish homes. Solar power, the most recent source of energy on Amish homesteads, is sometimes used to charge batteries, operate small electric motors, and charge electric fences.

The use of alternate power enables selective modernization while still respecting the ban on public electricity. Air and hydraulic power symbolize Amish self-sufficiency, reinforce separation from the world, and mark Amish identity. These alternate forms of "Amish electricity" are a creative compromise that preserves tradition in the midst of progress.

Selective Use of Technology

Popular images construe the Amish as organic farmers who milk their cows by hand. Although Lancaster's Amish do prefer the ways of nature, they certainly do not shun modern technology. Battery-powered, state-of-the-art LED lights, for example, are used on carriages and for many other applications around homes and shops. A wide array of technology increases efficiency and comfort in kitchens, barns, and shops. Technology is selectively used and sometimes harnessed in special ways.

Amish homemakers typically use dozens of common household items, including spray starch, detergents, instant pudding, disposable diapers, Ziploc bags, and permanent press fabrics, among others. Modern bathrooms, the latest gas appliances, and some pneumatic equipment are common in Amish households. Except for a few battery-powered gadgets, electrical appliances and lights are missing from Amish homes. Electric dryers and air conditioners are not found. Homes are normally heated by kerosene, coal, propane, or wood stoves.

A variety of technological improvements sustain farming operations— automatic milkers, tractors, elevators, welders, and electric cow trainers powered by batteries. Herbicides, insecticides, preservatives, and chemical fertilizers are widely used alongside modern veterinary practices. Although the Amish historically frowned upon artificial insemination of dairy cattle, the practice is now fairly widespread. But as discussed earlier, there are limits to acceptable farm technology.

Shops employ a vast array of mechanical equipment. Some craftsmen work with plastic and fiberglass materials. Small 12-volt motors, electrical inverters, and diesel engines energize shop equipment. Electronic cash registers, copiers, and word processors powered by inverters are commonplace. Computers and standard electrical equipment, with a few exceptions, are forbidden.

The telephone illustrates one example of the Amish struggle with technology. Forbidden inside homes, telephones are often found in "shanties" near shops, barns or houses. The phone was banned from homes about 1910, but its *use* was never forbidden. In the early decades of the twentieth century, Amish people often used the phones of neighbors or public telephones.

Battery-powered wheelchairs are widely used by the disabled. The steel-wheeled bench wagon in the background is used to transport benches to homes for church services.

Hoping to remain separate from the larger society, the Amish banned the telephone inside homes because it would tie them directly to the outside world. Strangers could freely enter Amish homes via the telephone. Besides, a ringing phone would disrupt the natural flow of family living, allowing outsiders to interrupt things at any moment. Face-to-face interaction and spontaneous visiting bond Amish society together. If one can call, then why visit?

In the 1940s, church leaders agreed to permit telephone "shanties" at the ends of farm lanes to call doctors and veterinarians, place feed orders, make appointments, and handle emergencies. These community phones, shared by several families, were primarily used for outgoing, rather than incoming, calls. As the number of Amish cottage industries grew in the 1980s, the telephone became necessary for ordering supplies and selling products. In the twenty-first century, phones remain banned inside homes, but most families have easy access to one—if not on their property, then at an Amish neighbor's.

Cell phones have created ongoing discussions. Some church districts permit them for contractors or other business owners, but the phones are not to be brought home. Young people sometimes purchase cell phones before they join the church. Gradually these phones are slipping into use, but they are still on probation, especially with their potential for wireless access to the Internet, which is firmly taboo.

Selective use of telephones is a way of mastering technology, of using it without becoming enslaved to it. Technology is restricted by the Amish when its long-term consequences appear to threaten the welfare of the community. New forms of technology are not thought of as sinful or evil; rather, they are tagged as worldly, unwise, too handy, or simply unnecessary, meaning they are considered a menace to the spiritual and social welfare of the community.

~

Civic Participation

Religious convictions govern Amish interactions with the larger society. Extensive participation in mainstream society not only would violate the tenets of religious separation, but also might eventually dissolve the boundaries that preserve Amish identity. Despite some restrictions, however, many Amish people develop congenial friendships with neighbors and non-Amish business associates. And for the most part, the Amish are good neighbors.

Amish persons also interact freely with outsiders via occupational roles—in retail shops, at farmers markets, and as waitresses in restaurants. Some Amish women develop long-term friendships with non-Amish employers while working as domestic aides in private homes. The ties are pleasant, but they do not flower into romantic relationships. Such relationships, to use biblical language, would be considered "unequal yoking" with unbelievers.

Amish participation in outside organizations is selective, informal, and locally oriented. Members typically do not join service clubs (Rotary, Kiwanis, Lions), country clubs, swimming pool associations, Boy Scouts or Girl Scouts of America, Little League teams, or community organizations such as the American Red Cross. Membership in professional and business organizations is also discouraged. Some farmers have joined the Dairy Herd Improvement Association, although not in all church districts. Those who do join the association are careful not to have their achievements publicized. In some communities, Amish

Amish and non-Amish join together at this civic event to raise funds for victims of poverty in Haiti.

men actively participate in volunteer fire companies. In fact, more than half of the members of some Lancaster County fire companies are Amish. The Amish also support fire companies through their public benefit auctions, which have annual sales topping several hundred thousand dollars.

Amish folks readily help their non-Amish neighbors in times of disaster, fire, or illness. Carpentry crews frequently travel out of state by bus or van under the auspices of the Mennonite Disaster Service or similar church agencies to rebuild homes destroyed by flood, hurricane, or tornado. Lancaster's Amish made many trips to assist in the reconstruction of homes in Mississippi following Hurricane Katrina in 2005. Church members also support benefit auctions, garage sales, and historical celebrations in the larger community. Every year, dozens of church districts provide volunteer labor for the Mennonite Central Committee and Christian Aid Ministries, packing supplies to aid international refugees devastated by war or famine.

Participation in carnivals, dances, and theaters is strongly forbidden for church members, although some families do visit attractions such as Hersheypark or the Philadelphia Flower Show. Cautious participation in civic affairs honors the age-old principle of separation from the world, reinforces the lines of Amish identity, and funnels social interaction through ethnic networks.

Government, Voting, and Taxes

The Amish view government with ambivalence. Although they support and respect civil government, they also keep a healthy distance from it. On the one hand, they follow biblical admonitions to obey and pray for rulers. Church leaders encourage members to be law-abiding citizens. On the other hand, government symbolizes worldly culture and the use of force. European persecutors of the Anabaptists were often government officials. Moreover, governments engage in warfare, use capital punishment, and impose their will with raw coercion. Believing that coercion mocks the gentle spirit of Jesus, the Amish reject the use of force, including litigation.

The church forbids membership in political organizations and public office holding. Holding political office is objectionable for several reasons. First, running for office violates Amish values of humility and modesty. Second, office holding compromises the religious principle of separation from the world. Finally, public officials must be prepared to use legal force if necessary to settle civic disputes. In Amish eyes, the exercise of legal force conflicts with biblical principles of nonresistance and nonviolence.

Voting, however, is viewed as a personal matter. The church has never prohibited it, but the number of Amish voters is typically low. Amish voters tend to favor Republican candidates. Republican leaders in Lancaster County made special efforts to register Amish voters in the 2004 presidential election. An unusually high number of eligible Amish adults, about 13 percent, cast ballots in that election. Joining political parties, attending political conventions, and campaigning for candidates fly in the face of the Amish virtues of simplicity, humility, and separation from the world.

When civil law and religious conscience collide, the Amish are not afraid to take a stand and, in biblical language, "obey God rather than man," even if it brings imprisonment. They have clashed with government officials over lights on carriages, zoning regulations, workers' compensation, and building codes for schools. As conscientious objectors, many received farm deferments or participated in alternative-service programs during times of military draft.

Government subsidies, or what the Amish call "handouts," have been stridently opposed by church leaders. Championing self-sufficiency and the separation of church and state, the Amish worry that the hand that feeds them will also control them. Over the years, they have stubbornly refused direct subsidies—even for agricultural programs designed for farmers in distress. Amish farmers do, however, receive indirect subsidies through agricultural price-support programs.

Following biblical injunctions, the Amish pay all taxes, except Social Security. Like other Americans, they pay federal and state income taxes, sales taxes, real estate taxes, and personal property taxes. Indeed, they pay school taxes twice—for both public and Amish schools. Because they make scant use of motor vehicles they pay little gasoline tax.

Unlike other Americans, the Amish do not pay Social Security taxes. They view Social Security as national government insurance, rather than a tax. The Amish object to government aid for several reasons. The church, they contend, should assume responsibility for the social welfare of its own members. The

The community frequently holds benefit auctions to assist families with large medical bills, because the Amish are not covered by commercial health insurance or Social Security. The products at this auction, made in Amish shops, were contributed to benefit a needy family.

aged, infirm, senile, mentally and physically disabled are cared for within extended family networks whenever possible. To turn the care of these folks over to the state would violate a fundamental tenet of faith—the care of one's brothers and sisters in the church.

Most church members neither pay into nor collect the benefits of Social Security. In 1965, Congress exempted self-employed persons who objected to Social Security for religious reasons. Amish employed in Amish businesses are also exempted by congressional legislation. Amish working in non-Amish businesses must pay Social Security, however, even though they do not reap its benefits. Paying Social Security without collecting benefits feels, in the words of one Amish man, "like buying a dead horse."

Bypassing Social Security not only severs the Amish from retirement payments, but also closes access to Medicare and Medicaid. The Amish worry that federal aid in the form of Social Security or Medicare would undercut church programs of mutual aid. They have organized several programs of mutual aid to assist members with fire and storm damages as well as with medical expenses.

The Amish have a long history of caring for their own and thus have little need for public welfare. They can hardly be called freeloaders or social parasites. On the whole, they tap few public funds. Indeed, by paying their fair share of taxes and siphoning off few public dollars, they not only take care of their own, but also make significant contributions to the public good.

Tourism

European forebears of the Amish were violently persecuted for daring to be different. Today the Amish defiance of modern culture brings admiration and respect—enough to underwrite a massive tourist industry. Indeed, tourism is Pennsylvania's second-largest industry, trailing only agriculture. Ironically, the world that the Amish have tried so hard to keep at bay now reaches out to them.

An Amish farmer traces the rise of Lancaster County tourism to the two hundredth birthday of the village of Intercourse in 1954: "Mix together the word *intercourse* and some Amish buggies," he says, "and you're bound to attract some tourists." An estimated 8.3 million tourists visit Lancaster county annually—about 300 visitors for each Amish person—and spend more than $1.5 billion. Although visitors come to Lancaster County for many reasons, the Amish are certainly a major magnet.

Tourism is often a nuisance to the Amish but sometimes a source of humor. Stories abound of visitors asking Amish people for directions to the Amish Vil-

Two boys ride their scooters on a backcountry road. This scene is one of many that beckons tourists to Lancaster County.

lage—assuming that Amish people live in a self-contained village; or of visitors' ignorance of the correct names of male and female animals, and so forth. Cars and buses clog country roads. Clicking cameras, gawking strangers, and incessant questions become tiresome. One Amish woman says, "We are opposed to having our souls marketed by having our sacred beliefs and traditions stolen from us and then distributed to tourists and sometimes mocked." In the words of an Amish minister, "The tourist attractions have converted our Amish land into a leisure lust playground."

Although tourism bothers the Amish soul, it also brings benefits. In recent years, hundreds of Amish roadside stands have sprung up, selling crafts, vegetables, and baked goods, among other things. These stands allow tourists a fleeting glimpse of Amish life and bring welcome revenues to Amish house-holds. The terms and times for interaction, however, are carefully regulated at a safe distance from Amish homes. Some Amish also operate retail furniture stores and quilt shops that target tourists. The Amish do not operate commercial enterprises that provide tours, programs, or exhibits for tourists, however.

Tourism brings more than economic benefits. In subtle ways, it bolsters collective self-esteem. An Amish statesman observes that with the rise of tourism, "We are no longer looked down upon." Says another member, "We get loads of praise for our way of life." Although reluctant to admit pride, the Amish enjoy a quiet satisfaction in knowing their culture is worthy of such interest and respect. Tourism also creates expectations for Amish behavior. To discard the horse and buggy would not only break Amish tradition, but also shatter the expectations placed on their community by outside visitors.

Perhaps most important, tourism fortifies Amish influence. Because they serve as a cultural magnet for tourism, the Amish have considerable political muscle when they negotiate with public officials over schools, highways, and zoning regulations. Thus in an ironic twist of history, these despised Old World heretics have become not only esteemed objects of curiosity, but influential in the political arena as well.

Amish and the Media

Clinging to the virtues of modesty and humility, the Amish have long deplored publicity and promotion. They object to photographs of themselves. To the Amish mind, personal portraits call attention to the individual and cultivate the sins of pride and vanity. By elevating individuals above the community, portraits exemplify the graven images condemned in the Bible's Ten Commandments. Moreover, the Amish eschew Hollywood movies because they spew the vulgarities of sex and violence around the world.

Amish coverage by print media began in the first half of the twentieth century. Media coverage increased dramatically in television and film in the last quarter of the twentieth century. The feature film *Witness*, with a cast of Amish characters, was widely viewed in the United States and abroad. Filmed in Lancaster County in the summer of 1984, *Witness* stirred controversy within the church. "We can't stop them," said one Amish man, "but we don't have to help them. We don't want it. It doesn't belong here."

Paramount solicited Amish help for staging and props, but church leaders made it clear that anyone aiding the project was liable for excommunication. Mistrust swelled with the discovery that actress Kelly McGillis had lived in disguise for several days in an Amish home.

Idyllic and pastoral images such as this one draw media attention to Amish life.

Members of the Amish community watched from afar as Harrison Ford, dressed in traditional garb, defended Amish ways with clenched fists in the village of Intercourse. The filming prompted church leaders to protest to Pennsylvania's lieutenant governor, as well as other state and local officials. Said one Amish man, "If our principles were to fight, I feel we could go to court and get an injunction on the basis of misrepresenting the Amish, but this is not our way."

The violence of a cop thriller framed by pastoral scenes of Amish countryside created a dramatic clash of images. Despite an implausible plot and some cultural errors, *Witness* did present a sensitive and fair interpretation of the Amish spirit.

Over the past twenty-five years, a television series, *Aaron's Way*, and several feature and made-for-TV films, such as *For Richer or Poorer, Plain Truth, Kingpin, Harvest of Fire*, and *Stoning in Fulham County*, have also depicted Amish life with various levels of authenticity. An HBO documentary about Amish young people, *Devil's Playground*, followed four rebellious teens during *Rumspringa* in Indiana. In the summer of 2004, in a five-episode reality television series called *Amish in the City*, CBS featured five Amish youths living with five worldly youths in a contemporary home in Los Angeles. Prior to the show's airing, CBS received many letters of protest, including a petition signed by fifty-one U.S. senators and representatives, led by Lancaster County representative Joe Pitts.

The Lancaster Amish also received significant national and international news coverage in 1998 when two Amish-raised youths were arrested for selling cocaine to other Amish young people. The story was sensational because the Amish drug dealers bought the drugs from members of the Pagans Motorcycle Club, with whom they worked at a construction site. The most extensive media coverage of the Amish occurred in the fall of 2006, when a non-Amish neighbor took ten girls hostage in an Amish schoolhouse in Lancaster County, killing five of them and seriously injuring the rest.

The Tragedy at Nickel Mines

On Monday, October 2, 2006, a tragic event shocked and distressed the Amish and the larger world as well. That morning, in Nickel Mines, about four miles southeast of Strasburg, a non-Amish neighbor walked into a one-room Amish school and took the children, their teacher, and a few visiting adults hostage. Charles Carl Roberts IV, a local tank truck driver, picked up milk from Amish and English farms in the area. There was no previous hostility between Roberts and Amish families, and no evidence that he targeted the children because they were Amish. Unknown to anyone, however, he had been planning to molest children for several weeks and likely selected schoolchildren because they were

The New Hope Amish school at Nickel Mines opened on April 2, 2007, exactly six months after the tragedy.

An Amish craftsman created this wood plaque as a gift for the Pennsylvania State Police. The surviving pupils signed their names with a wood-burning pencil.

easy targets. He had purchased supplies, including three guns, necessary for a lengthy standoff with police.

Soon after Roberts arrived at the school, the teacher escaped and ran to a nearby Amish farmhouse for help. The farmer called 911 to report that a man was holding the twenty-six pupils hostage. Eventually Roberts dismissed all of the boys and the adult visitors from the schoolhouse. He began barricading the doors and windows shut and forced the girls to lie facedown on the floor at the front of the room. He then tied some of their legs together. When police arrived in the schoolyard, he became agitated and called 911 to demand that everyone clear the property within two seconds or he would begin shooting.

Shortly thereafter, he shot the ten girls, aged six to thirteen, execution style, killing five and seriously wounding the others. As police stormed the schoolroom, Roberts shot himself. The horrific event was soon reported by news media around the world. Reporters followed the story for five days, until the children and their killer were buried.

The event stunned the world, but the Amish response to it shocked observers even more. Within hours of the shooting, before the sun had set on that awful October day, various Amish people began extending expressions of forgiveness to the killer's widow and family. The swift Amish response of forgiveness, instead of rage, startled the world. Within a week of the shooting, more than 2,400 news stories in many countries featured the forgiving Amish response. Indeed, in the days following the tragedy, the story of Amish forgiveness overshadowed the shooting itself in the worldwide media. The horrific event received more news coverage than any other event in Amish history. "Our forgiveness," says an Amish father, "meant that we chose not to hold a grudge against the widow and the killer's family."

Six months to the day, on April 2, 2007, the Amish opened the New Hope School for the surviving children at Nickel Mines. Four of the injured girls had recovered and were attending school. One, however, remained at home because of her injuries. The tragic event brought the Amish and their English neighbors closer together. In countless ways, the police, civic officials, and Amish worked hand in hand to respond to the tragic event in the days and months that followed. The Nickel Mines Amish community and the gunman's family also renewed and strengthened their friendship, a relationship made possible in part by the surprising expression of Amish forgiveness.

~

Art and Creative Expression

Amish culture has historically eschewed public artistic expression. Several strands of their religious heritage have stifled the artistic spirit. Members of the Anabaptist movement disdained the images and art of the state churches in Europe. They viewed these works of art as idolatry, equivalents of the biblically forbidden graven images.

Moreover, individualistic artistic expression collides with the communal values of Amish culture. Such expression, in the Amish mind, breeds pride and exalts the individual. In the past, homemade Amish dolls were typically faceless to avoid the appearance of graven images and erase individual expression.

Amish culture is also rooted in the soil of practical rural values. To rural farmers, eking out a living by the sweat of their brows, art is a waste of time, impractical and frivolous. Pragmatic and useful activities are treasured in Amish

An Amish woman uses this worktable to create crafts and dried flower arrangements for sale.

culture, but not the fantasies of individual artists. The Amish want to know if something works; is it practical and useful?

Despite these restraints, some expressions of folk art have bubbled out of Amish life over the centuries. Barbara Ebersole (1864–1922) was widely known for her *Fraktur,* lovely artistic lettering with fancy hearts, tulips, and other flowers. She designed colorful bookplates for Bibles and other family records, and her designs now top $3,000 at public auctions. Embroidered family registers, calendars, and genealogical charts have long decorated Amish walls. Quilt designs, garden flowers, and homemade crafts are age-old forms of artistic expression.

In recent years, the usefulness of Amish art has grown as Amish craft sales have soared. Art has suddenly become practical for making a living in the face of diminishing farmland. A wide spectrum of artistic expression has blossomed in crafts, but it remains folk art. Saws, shingles, metal discs, and other practical items are painted by hand. Needlework, corn-husk dolls, and quilts galore are just some of hundreds of items produced and sold by the Amish.

One artist complains that "it's okay to paint milk cans but not to display your work at art shows." But even that is changing. Some self-trained Amish artists are beginning to paint on canvas as well as to display and sell their work. One Amish artist was even featured in *USA Today*. An exhibit of Amish art appeared in the Lancaster region for the first time in the early 1990s.

Church leaders have permitted such ventures, especially for members with financial needs, when the art clearly involves making a living. But the emerging art remains encased in cultural patterns. The pastoral scenes on canvas are limited to depictions of actual Amish settings. Individual images are rarely drawn, and when they are, faces are never shown.

Dying Gracefully

A Lancaster-area funeral director observes that the Amish accept death in graceful ways. With the elderly living at home, the gradual loss of health prepares family members for the final passage. Accompanied by quiet grief, death comes gracefully, as the final benediction to a good life and entry into the bliss of eternity. Funeral preparations reflect the core Amish values of simplicity, humility, and mutual aid, as family and friends yield to eternal verities.

The community springs into action at the word of a death. Family and friends assume barn, business, and household chores, freeing the immediate family. Three couples are appointed to extend invitations to the funeral and supervise activities—food preparation, seating arrangements, and the coordination of a large number of horses and carriages.

Well-established funeral rituals unburden the family from difficult funeral choices. A non-Amish undertaker moves the body to a funeral home for embalming. The body, with minimal cosmetic improvements and dressed in long underwear, returns to the home in a simple wooden coffin within a day. Family members dress the body in white. A deceased woman often wears the white cape and apron she wore at her wedding. Tailoring the white clothes prior to death helps prepare the family for the season of grief. White garments symbolize the final passage into a new and better eternal life.

Friends and relatives visit the family and view the body in a bedroom on the first floor of the home for two days prior to the funeral. Meanwhile, community members dig the grave by hand in a nearby family cemetery as others oversee the daily chores of the bereaved. Several hundred guests attend the funeral in a barn, shop, or home, typically on the morning of the third day after death. During the simple hour-and-a-half service, ministers read hymns and scriptures, offer prayers, and preach a sermon. Singing and eulogies are

Most Amish people die at home surrounded by extended family. It's not unusual for two or three generations to live side by side on the same homestead.

missing, and there are no flowers, burial gowns, burial tents, limousines, or sculpted monuments.

The hearse, a large, black carriage pulled by horses, leads a long procession of other carriages to the burial ground on the edge of a farm. A brief viewing and graveside service mark the return of "dust to dust." Pallbearers lower the coffin and shovel soil into the grave as an ordained leader reads a hymn. Small, equal-size tombstones indicate the places of the deceased in the community of equality. After the service, close friends and family members return to the home for a meal.

Following a death, bereaved women who lost a close relative signal their mourning by wearing a black dress in public settings for as long as a year. A painful separation laced with grief, death is nevertheless received gracefully as the ultimate surrender to God's higher ways. With the bereaved surrounded by family and friends, and comforted by predictable rituals filled with religious meanings, the separation is humane by modern standards. Tears flow, but the sobs are restrained—quiet submission acknowledging the rhythms of divine purpose. From cradle to grave, the mysteries of life and death unravel in the context of loving families and supportive rituals.

Related Religious Groups

The Amish are one of more than two dozen religious groups in Lancaster County with Anabaptist roots. There are three other horse-and-buggy driving groups, all of which are part of the Mennonite family. The Stauffer Mennonites, nicknamed "Pikers" because their meetinghouse is along an old turnpike, have one congregation in Lancaster County. The Reidenbach Mennonites, known locally as "Thirty-Fivers," have several congregations. The largest group that uses buggy transportation is the Wenger Mennonites, sometimes called the "Team" Mennonites. They have ten meetinghouses in Lancaster County.

All of these Old Order Mennonite groups differ from the Amish in several ways. Their carriages are black, whereas Amish carriages are gray. Unlike the

The Old Order Wenger Mennonites drive black carriages. The vinyl covering on Amish carriages is always gray. The carriage body and wheels are typically made from fiberglass.

Amish, who hold church services in their homes, the Mennonites have meetinghouses. Mennonite men do not wear beards as Amish men do. Amish women wear plain-colored dresses, whereas the Mennonite women wear dresses made of patterned fabric.

The Wengers are the most progressive of the horse-and-buggy-driving Mennonite groups. Unlike the Amish, the Wengers use steel-wheeled tractors in the field, have telephones in their homes, and tap into the public utility grid for electricity in their homes and shops.

Despite these differences, the Amish and the Old Order Mennonites share many common practices. Most of the Mennonites are located in the northeastern section of Lancaster County, away from the Amish community. In areas where Mennonite and Amish communities overlap, however, they cooperate in operating private schools. Old Order Mennonites and Amish typically subscribe to the same correspondence newspapers, *Die Botschaft* and *The Diary*. These newspapers, written in English, are filled with letters of local news from scribes in various communities across the country.

The Beachy Amish and Amish Mennonite churches are more progressive cousins of the Amish. The Beachy Amish, a car-driving group, originated from the Amish in 1907. This group has seven meetinghouses in Lancaster County. There are also various Amish Mennonite congregations in the Lancaster area. Both the Beachy Amish and the Amish Mennonites are frequent recipients of Amish who leave their community for a more expressive form of religion and more access to technology. These groups dress plainly, but drive cars, use public electricity, and emphasize evangelistic meetings and missionary activity more than the Old Order Amish do.

Additional plain-dressing and car-driving Mennonite churches in Lancaster County include the Eastern Mennonite Church and the Horning Mennonite Church. The Hornings are sometimes called the "Black Bumper" Mennonites because in the mid-twentieth century, they painted the chrome on their cars black.

In addition to the plain-dressing churches, two large assimilated Anabaptist groups with congregations in Lancaster County are Mennonite Church USA and the Church of the Brethren. These churches total about 25,000 members, not including children. For the most part, they have accepted many mainstream cultural practices, such as wearing contemporary dress, owning televisions and computers, and using musical instruments in their worship services. Many of their members graduate from college and pursue professional occupations.

These diverse groups all grew out of the same religious heritage, but they have chosen different cultural expressions of their faith while continuing to share core religious convictions. The Amish are but one group in the colorful patchwork of Anabaptist-related churches in Lancaster County.

The Future of Amish Society

W hat will be the fate of Amish society? Will the Amish continue to ride in buggies and shun electricity throughout the twenty-first century? Might Lancaster's Amish migrate en masse to rural hideaways in other states or even other countries? Will sprawling suburbs devour Amish lands and change Amish life beyond recognition? Some scholars in the mid-1950s predicted the demise of Amish society. They were obviously wrong. Indeed, the Amish have flourished in the most technologically advanced period of history. But what about their future?

The future of Amish life defies prediction. New patterns of Amish culture will be shaped not only by external forces—market prices, government regulations, rates of urbanization—but also by challenges inside their communities. Although crystal-ball scenarios are tenuous at best, past practices may offer some clues to the future.

Three habits of the past will likely shape Amish responses to the future: high-density farming, alternative nonfarm work, and emigration. Despite high land prices and encroaching urbanization, a portion of Lancaster's Amish will probably continue to till the soil well into the twenty-first century. As one businessman says, "The Amish in Lancaster feel that Lancaster's our home; we don't move away as quickly as the Amish in other states." Farmland preservation programs, which the Amish support, as well as their emotional ties to their ancestral soil in the oldest North American Amish settlement, will continue to tether some to the land.

But farming practices will surely change. Large farms will continue to decline in size as more Amish develop specialized operations on smaller plots of land to raise produce for regional markets. Others will specialize in raising organic vegetables, organically grown chickens, exotic game animals, and pets for urban pet stores. Small specialty farming operations will likely grow in the future.

The willingness of many Amish to leave their plows for cottage industries in the 1980s signaled a dramatic change of direction. By the first decade of the twenty-first century, nearly 2,000 Amish-owned businesses were flourishing in Lancaster County. More than two-thirds of Amish households are involved in some type of business, and this trend will likely persist. As the small industries

The future of Amish society lies in the hands and minds of the rising generation.

bloom, they will bring many changes to Amish life, including greater use of technology and more interaction with the outside world. The business endeavors will slowly alter the egalitarian class structure of Amish society over the years. Economic and cultural divisions among farmers, day laborers, and entrepreneurs will likely grow.

Because the love of farming lies deep in the Amish heart, some families will likely migrate out of state in search of fertile soil at a reasonable price. Throughout their history, the Amish have readily moved in the face of persecution and adversity. Indeed, more than sixty congregations in several states trace their roots back to Lancaster. In recent decades, new settlements have been established in Indiana, Kentucky, New York, and Wisconsin. A sudden massive migration is unlikely, but steady dribbles of Lancaster emigrants to rural areas of the United States will surely continue.

The cultural flavor of twenty-first-century Amish life eludes forecast, but one emergent pattern is clear: Rural homesteads remain the best places to preserve traditional Amish ways. If the Amish can educate and retain their children, make a living without merchandising their souls, and restrain interaction with the larger world, they will probably flourish in the twenty-first century. But as they multiply, one thing is certain: They will continue to change, adapt, and shatter many of the staid stereotypes of their traditional life.

Index

Religion
  baptism, 10, 20, 44
  Bible, 15, 16, 18, 21, 70
  church congregations, 3, 5
  church/state separation, 65–67
  communion, 21, 36
  confession, public, 22, 23
  death, 23, 25, 30, 33, 77–79
  dropout rate, 5
  excommunication, 20, 22–23, 44
  holidays, 36–37
  ordination, 21
  Ordnung, 18–22, 44, 47–48
  outsiders and, 10
  prayer, 15, 16, 36, 40
  related groups, 12, 65, 79–81
  roots of Amish, 10–12
  shunning, 20, 22–23, 44
  spirituality, 15–17
  values, 12–15, 41
  weddings, 23, 33, 36, 44–46
  women, role of, 9, 20, 21, 27
  worship services, 2, 16, 33
  written sources, 15–18, 20, 21, 70
Rumspringa, 9, 36, 42–44, 72

Saws, power, 58, 59
Schools. *See* Education
Sewing machines, 60
Shunning, 20, 22–23, 44
Simplicity, 13, 15, 51, 66
Skates, in-line, 7, 9, 18
Social life
  See also Marriage; Religion
  barn raisings, 25, 35
  benefit auctions, 25, 25
  community life described, 23–25
  harvesting, 25
  holidays, 36–37

Solar power, 60
Stoning in Fulham County, 72
Stoves, 60
Submission, 12–13, 22

Taxes, 66–67
Telephones, 7, 9, 80
  cell phones, 18, 63
  history of selective use, 61–63
Television(s), 6, 9, 18, 22, 32, 40, 58,
    59, 81
  Amish portrayed by, 42, 70–71
Theater, 65
Tourism, 68–70
Tractors, 9, 22, 56–58, 61, 80

Values, 12–15, 41
VCRs, 58
Voting, 66

Washing machines, 60
Welders, electric, 58, 59, 61
Wengers, 80
Windmills, 8
Witness, 71–72
Women, role of
  birth, 23, 25, 27–28
  in business, 9, 35, 52–53
  employed by non-Amish, 63–64
  in family, 27, 53
  in religion, 9, 20, 21, 27
  as teachers, 27
  weddings, 23, 33, 36, 44–46
Work ethic, 14–15, 75

Youth
  See also Education
  decision to join the church, 20, 44
  Rumspringa, 9, 36, 42–44, 72

About the Author and the Photographer

Donald B. Kraybill is a distinguished professor at Elizabethtown College and senior fellow at the Young Center for Anabaptist and Pietist Studies. He has studied and written widely on the Amish and other Anabaptist groups of North America. For more information, visit www.etown.edu/Amishstudies.

Daniel Rodriguez is a freelance photographer who lives in Elizabethtown, Pennsylvania. His photos of the Plain communities have appeared in a variety of books and other publications.